Introdu

CW00522352

Prior to retiring from the farm, Roy   ~~~ about his childhood and his years spent farming in Fletching. He put pen to paper and these are the results! They were originally published in Fletching Parish Magazine.

These are all Roy's memories, but we all know that memory sometimes plays tricks so we accept that there may be some readers who recall certain events somewhat differently!

About the Author

Roy Pendennis Lingham was born on 23rd May 1922 at Ashurst Wood, near East Grinstead, Sussex. His parents were Gwendolene and Donald Lingham who farmed Woolpack Farm, Fletching.

In 1934 Roy moved to Vigoes Farm, Sheffield Green, farming it as a tenant farmer until the Estate was broken up in 1954. He then bought Vigoes and continued to farm there until he retired in 2001 and moved to Newick.

He had lived in Fletching Parish for 79 years.

A true village gentleman.

ACKNOWLEDGMENTS

The photograph of **Fletching Home Guard Christmas Dinner** is reproduction by kind permission of Edward Reeves (Lewes) ©.

All other photographs are from Roy Lingham's private collection.

Sheffield Park Railway Station

NOVEMBER 2000

This was quite a busy little station when I used to travel to and fro the school at East Grinstead. I had a few friends go with me: they were David Claridge from the Post Office at Fletching, Steve Bentley from the Griffin Hotel, Roger Mepham from Flitteridge Farm, Jack Pickwell from the Park, whose father was chauffeur to Captain Soames, and Mary Burns from Rock Cottage, Furners Green. We used to catch the 8.30 hrs. and return on the one that arrived at 18.00 hrs.

On week-days about 10 o'clock the goods train would be shunted into the goods yard to trucks of coal, etc. At that time there would be two passenger trains in the station, one on the way to London and one to Brighton. After they had gone, the goods train would travel to East Grinstead, via Horsted Keynes, West Hoathly and Kingscote; it would have to return by 14.00 hrs. as there would be another two passenger trains due. It would then go on to Newick, Barcombe and Lewes.

Three Coal Merchants used the goods yard; Mr. Bentley of Fletching, Mr. Emmens of Nutley and Mr. Coates of Danehill.

Turners Timber Merchants had a special branch line into their yard and in the Autumn several farmers had sheep sent to them on cattle trucks. They came from the marshes and were kept until the Spring. It was quite something for us boys to help drive them to their winter quarters – Mr. Perkins, the Station Master, was always glad to see the back of us boys!!

Sussex Barns

NOVEMBER 2000

Just how many of the old Sussex Barns have we lost in the Parish? Here are just a few that I can remember, starting with the one in the opposite side of Woolpack Farm that has now gone and the one at Stephens Farm that was on the north of Sheffield Forest. There was a barn and closed-in yard at Coleham and there was also a built-in Shepherd's Hut, where sometimes tramps would spend the night on their way from workhouse to workhouse. There was Tricklands Barn, Yard and Hovel, and also New Barn at Ketches Farm which was on the South side of Kings Wood, and a small one opposite Spring Farm; also one at Clapwater.

There are a few that have now be made into houses: Sheffield Mill Farm, Ketches Home Farm, Northall Farm, Spring Farm.

The Barn at Pound Farm is now no more; but whatever happened to the one that was in the middle of Vigoes Farm I shall never know. The pond is still there, so is the mark where the horse used to walk round and round to drive the machinery.

Express Dairy Returns

At Sheffield Park there was a small Dairy known as the Mid-Sussex Creamery in the 1920s, where most of the local farmers sent their milk. Those farmers who lived close by took their milk in churns (17 gallon ones) by horse and cart. Those living further away had theirs brought in by small lorries, these being owned by Mr. Terry who collected in the Newick area, Mr. Awcock in the Danehill and Chelwood Gate areas, and Mr. Lingham from Woolpack Farm the Nutley and Fletching areas.

Those who worked in the Dairy were, as I remember, Mr. Bray, the Manager, Bill Watson in the office, and Tom Dubber, Frank Marten, Harry Watson, Ted Clarkson and Percy Simons.

It was in the mid-thirties that the Express Dairy took over and they soon closed it down; all the milk had to be taken to their other depot at Horam. This, of course, meant that the workers had to find other jobs, most of them going to Turner's Timber Yard, except Bill Watson who started his own milk round delivery in Lewes. It also meant that no more milk would be sent away in churns from Sheffield Park Station, from where it used to go to London and the South Coast.

When the Second World War started, the Dairy had been empty for some time, but then the Express Dairy sent down from the London HQ a Manager and four lady staff members who lodged at various places in Sheffield Park: the Manager, Mr. Odell, and his wife at Pound Farm; two of the ladies at Trickland Cottages; one with Mr. and Mrs. Setford at The Forge; and Mr. Odell's daughter, who was married to John Erwin, lived at Fletching.

After the War ended, the Dairy became empty again as the milk from the local farms was then collected by lorries owned by the Milk Marketing Company. For a few years the Dairy remained empty, until Mrs. Sales, a lady from Danehill who had a small retail milk round, bought it and began buying milk from local farmers, bottling it and delivering it locally. She gradually expanded, collecting more milk and selling it in Haywards Heath, East Grinstead and Crowborough. This small Dairy then became too small and a much larger one was built on the opposite side of the A275. Now the old Dairy is derelict and the new one is expanding so much that it is taken over again by the Express Dairy Company.

Sheffield Arms Hotel

JANUARY 2001

We moved next to the Hotel on 29th March, 1934 and found that our new neighbours were Mr. and Mrs. Edwards and their son, Frank. They had quite a good many guests and a very good saloon and public bar trade, and Mrs. Edwards used to do the Teas when Sheffield Park Garden was open to the public; tea was held in the Pavilion on the Sheffield Park Cricket Ground.

The next couple to take the Arms were Mr. and Mrs. Hayes; then came Mr. and Mrs. Swaby. The Swabys went soon after the War started and Mr. and Mrs. Grace took over. As the cry "Dig for Victory" came, this meant the grass tennis court and the bowling green had to be ploughed up for potatoes. They (that is Mr. and Mrs. Grace) stayed until 1948 and after them came a series of Managers: Mr. Sutton, Mr. Kimberley, Mr. Salmone, Mr. Sargent and Mr. Wake. Mr. and Mrs. Wake left to take over the Rose & Crown, and in came Mr. and Mrs. Clayson who stayed for nine years, until Mr. Clayson died of cancer. After that there was one more tenant before the 99-year lease (held by Tamlins Brewery) ran out; the Arms was then empty for 18 months. It was sold to Halland Motels Company who got planning consent to construct a Motel at the rear of the Sheffield Arms. They went bankrupt. There were more owners who were all going to do great things but they, too, finished up losing money. Now the Arms is owned by Mr. and Mrs. Clifford, who deal in Indian furniture.

Keepers of the Sheffield Park Estate

When the Sheffield Estate was sold in 1954, that was the end of the Pheasant Shooting and the employment of the Keepers.

The first Head Keeper I can remember was Mr. Pritchard, who lived in Walkwood Cottage. The staff under him were Mr. Burley and his son Maurice, Fred Lucas, Jim Norton (the Estate's Blacksmith's son), Mr. Ted Holmes and a young man they called Silver, and Mr. Dancy. Their main work was the rearing of pheasants. This meant that they collected the eggs from those hen pheasants that had been kept in pens, from nests that were found on the farms of the Estate, and also from nests found by the tenants and their workers (payment a few pence a nest). The Keepers were then stationed in the Estate woods, with nest boxes close by, each box with about 16 eggs and a hen to hatch them (3 weeks). Every day the hens had to be taken off the eggs to be fed and watered and, so that they kept to their own boxes, each hen had a piece of string tied to one leg and stumped to the ground. When the eggs hatched, the small chicks and the mother hen were then transferred to coops, then taken to an adjoining field and spaced about 10 yards apart. They stayed like that for several weeks until the chicks could do without the mother hen. Then they were taken back into the wood so that as they grew they would eventually roost in the trees.

Come the Autumn, it was time for the Gentry to start their sport, pheasant shooting. Those birds that were out in the fields had to be driven into the wood and kept there until the guns were placed around the wood at one side; then the keepers and beaters drove the birds towards the guns so that they either flew away or got shot. The dead birds were collected and put in the game cart (driven by Fred Wood) as the guns and keepers moved on to the next wood.

When the shoot was let to Lord Glendyne of East Grinstead, in partnership with the Sheffield Park Estate, Mr. Richardson became the next Head Keeper. You may wonder what happened to Mr. Pritchard – well, that is another story! I am not quite sure of the facts and must talk to Mr. Fred Gladman who was, at that time, an apprentice keeper under Mr. Pritchard.

The Home Guard

In May 1940 the Local Defence Volunteers first took action, by forming a night patrol to watch the sky for paratroops. Soon after, it became the Home Guard. We were D Company, part of 17th Battalion, Sussex Home Guard (East Grinstead). In charge was Major Henricks and our platoon came under Cpt. Tremlet, who was the Agent for the Sheffield Park Estate.

Our Night guards were held in the Reading Room at Sheffield Green, from 20.00 hrs. until 6.00 hrs. the next morning. Usually there were five Privates and an NCO doing guard duty, two of the men being stationed outside, watching and stopping people and checking their identity. On Sunday mornings there was drill, either in the Park or at the railway station which we might have had to defend in the event of enemy action. Sometimes the regular Army took us to Old Lodge in Ashdown Forest, for rifle practise as they had a proper range there. We also had a small range of our own in the old brickyard at Sheffield Green, where we practised with .22 rifles, sten guns and Tommy guns, not forgetting revolvers. It was in the Park that we learned to throw hand grenades and Molotov cocktails. Other training included first aid, gas alert, aircraft recognition, map reading and RT and Field telephone; also how to strip down Bren guns, Vickers machine guns and Spigot mortars.

At Christmas 1943 we had a Dinner given by the Landlord and his wife (Mr. and Mrs. Harry Grace) at the Sheffield Arms Hotel.

The photograph was taken by Private Edward Reeves and the following names are of those in the photo.

Private Edward Reeves, of Edward Reeves (Lewes), photographers, was the father of the present owner.

C. Burrows   W. Pyke   F. Wood   W. Baker   E. Barker

W. Burley   C. Barker   W. Richardson   F. Baker   V. Slarkes

J. Marchant   C. Brazer   F. Richardson   J. Weller   J. Maclean

J. Jager   F. Martin   B. Mellows   B. Wood   A. Palmer

J. Sandalls   D. Neeves   G. Wilkens   M. Chapman   R. Lingham

S. Pitman   C. Beard   Major Henricks   R. Diplock   R. Whiting

R. Willey   Capt. Tremlet   E. Padgham   W. Ockenden   J. Sandalls

Roy Lingham is second on the left

Fletching Home Guard Christmas Dinner 1943

held at the Sheffield Arms

©Edward Reeves (Lewes)

The Home Guard Again

MAY 2001

Thinking back, here are just a few of the funny things that happened (Dad's Army!) We were being marched up towards the railway station with a Sergeant in charge (Mr. Slarkes, who was a Carter on the Estate). Suddenly we were given the command "Whoa, get back". He must have thought we were horses! One night patrol we had marched up to Furners Green, down Sliders Lane and back to the Reading Room via Ketches Farm. When we were paraded for dismissal we found we had lost a Private; but it was all right – he had slipped off at Ketches to look at his rabbit wires. He came into the pub later on with half-a- dozen! One Sunday morning while we were having instruction on firing a Spigot mortar, Private Fred Crowhurst raised the elevation to 'high', thus cutting through the electric cables and putting the whole Army camp in Sheffield Park out of action.

When we were first issued with a few Sten guns we were taught how to strip them down and re-assemble them; then we went to a range at The Brickyard to fire single shots at a cut-out figure, holding the gun at our hip. One soldier happened to slip the gun into automatic, thus firing off 28 rounds in a few seconds. Instead of pointing the gun to the ground, he lifted it into the air; the bullets flew through the trees at Trickland and the Sentries dived for cover! During one training exercise we left two men behind to cook us a meal for our return. It was different. In the mobile copper was a meat and vegetable stew boiling away and in the stew was some jam roly-poly pudding! Yes, it certainly tasted different.

Bombs dropped: incendiaries at Woolpack Farm – 2 through the house roof, 15 around the building, some close to the hay stacks and the rest in the wood on the opposite side of the road. Two HE in the Park, 2 HE at Furners Green. A stick of HEs* starting at Searles and finishing at Northall Farm. Two at Flitteridge Farm. A V1 or Doodlebug at Pound Farm, killing one horse and injuring another which had to be put down; six bullocks which were lying down closer to where it hit the ground escaped unhurt, as the blast went over them.

There was damage to the houses and buildings close by and Mrs. Wood, who lived at Winter Cottage, was trapped in bed with the ceiling down on top of her; she was rescued by the ARP* Warden.

Roy outside Vigoes Farm 1941

*HE - High Explosive

*ARP - Air Raid Precaution

More on the Home Guard

JUNE 2001

These planes were shot down in the area: a ME109 in Bell Lane, Tinker Wood; a Wellington at Nutley; a Spitfire and two Typhoons at Piltdown; a B17 close to the recreation ground at Fletching; and another Typhoon near Danehill.

There was a little song we used to sing:

"Us Home Guards here have never been in action as before
But when we do, we promise you there'll never be any more War.
We will capture all the Italians, the Germans and the Japs,
And make the blighters do our work, while we sit back and relax."

There was a Searchlight Unit in a field close to the Fletching Road between Northall Farm and Vigoes Farm; it was composed of the Light plus Radar, a Lister Engine to drive the Light and two gun pits, one with twin Browning guns and one with a Lewes gun. There were two large huts hidden in the straw, one for sleeping and the other, as well as being the cook house and rest room, was where we ate our meals. A small hut was the toilet and wash room. Those who looked after the Light were a Sergeant, a Corporal, and about eight Privates, all belonging to the Royal Artillery.

When the War started, the searchlight was first put close to the Shop at Furners Green and the troops lived under canvas for a few months. Then it was moved to its permanent position and remained there until we crossed the Rhine, when the troops were moved to Germany. They were here for about four years and got to know all the locals; they used the Sheffield Arms a good deal and even had a field telephone laid on, so that, if a warning or "Take Post" came through, they could get back to the Light very quickly.

As far as I know, they only fired their guns at the enemy once, when seven FW190s* came over very low, heading back to the coast.

If and when the boys had some spare time, they would give a hand on the farms, haying, harvesting, swede and mangold hoeing, even a bit of hedge cutting; and when they went on leave they usually were able to take home a few eggs or a rabbit and some vegetables. After the war finished, for many years they used to come back and see us when they had their holidays.

*FW - Focke-Wulf

Sheffield Green

JULY 2001

The Green, as I know it, is the piece of land in front of the Sheffield Arms with its seven oaks and two chestnut trees, where they used to hold an annual Fair and side shows and races on the opposite side of the road.

This land on each side of the A275 up to Furners Green we called the Common, but it was not so and was really Manorial Waste, looked after by the current Lord of the Manor. It extended from Lane End to the Red Lion at Chelwood Gate. There were, I know, three old Notice boards stating this fact: one amongst the trees on the Green, another halfway up the Common in a clump of fir trees and the last one close to the telephone box at Paygate.

The tenants of Vigoes and Pound Farms were allowed to graze their cows on the Common. Mr. Tester's two boys, Jack and Bill, looked after their cows on the West side of the road, and I looked after ours on the East side, mostly before going to, or after, school. There were quite a few of us young boys who used to play on the Common, and come November the Fifth we would have a bonfire and a few bangers opposite Chequers, where Jack and Tom Dubber lived.

Sometimes the gypsies stayed with their caravans and horses, but after a few days they were moved on by the local police – Mr. Mead of Fletching and Mr. Patten of Danehill.

The gypsies knew all the tricks. After dark they would put their horses in one of the fields close by and in Winter take some hay to feed them; they would also take milk and potatoes and a little corn for the few chickens they had. I have seen them move off to their next place to stay, with the hens roosting on the back axle and their Lurcher dog trotting along behind (these dogs were very good for catching rabbits). They would also take a long pole, tie a loop of wire to it and slip it around a pheasant's neck as it roosted in the trees.

Roy Lingham Remembers

The time has come for me to lay down my pen. I never thought that I could write these things for the Parish Magazine, though for many years I have been asked to do so.

Well, now comes a very sad part of my life: my first home (Woolpack Farm) is to be sold and so is my second, Vigoes Farm. Seventy-nine years I have lived in Fletching Parish – not quite true, as I was away for a little while at the beginning of the second War, not really of my own choosing.

I have seen so many changes that it is not possible to write about them all. Firstly, the change in farming. When I was a boy all the farms had a few cows and the horses did all the work; it used to be my job to take our horses down to the Blacksmith's at Splaynes Green to be shod. When it came to haymaking and harvest time, everyone came to help and Father always had a barrel of cider to refresh the workers. Nowadays it is all done by tractor and machinery (no fun at all); most times in the pub we talked about how many loads we had done, all trying to outdo the other farms (all good fun).

Now when I go through the Village it is so different. Yes, the pubs are there, but not the same; people come from miles around for meals, not like it was. All the shops have gone, except the Butcher's and that has moved to the other side of the house; no slaughterhouse now, all the meat comes in lorries. It is a good job that Graham is a good Butcher and buys in the best meats. No Post Office and we all have to go into town for our groceries; we used to put our order in and it was delivered to our door. I can remember Mr. Moore coming up to Woolpack on his bike with the letters and papers, and Mr. Grover coming with the horse and trap with the meat. You know, we could get our boots and shoes mended, also our clothes sewn and repaired, at little places up the street and, of course, we did not have to go out of the village for a Doctor.

Still, the School is there, but not all the children of the village go to it, although I think it is a good school and all the teachers take a lot of pride in their work. Mr. Dudley Martin does a fine thing to arrange the reunion for us, just to meet up once a year.

I hope that my articles have been of some use and that I have not offended too many people.

I, for one, have enjoyed Roy's articles enormously, as I am sure have many other readers. Thank you, Roy, very much. We are all sad that you and your family are leaving Vigoes Farm. Roy has written a few poems about Village people and happenings and over the next few months I hope to be able to print some of them.

Editor

Flight Sergeant R. P. Lingham

SEPTEMBER 2001

It must have been over sixty years ago
That I got the call, to the RAF to go
Doing basic training like all the rest,
Then becoming an Air Gunner was the best.
Passing out, getting my half wing,
Then fourteen days, was just the thing.
Returning back for my very first Op,
The nerves were going; I thought they would pop.
The green light flashed and off we went,
Thinking of the leave that I'd just spent.
Over the sea and then the coast ahead,
How I wished that I was still in bed.
Sitting alone in the turret at the back
Now there are pretty lights – it must be flak.
The Skipper shouted: "Target ahead,
Look out for fighters, Roy and Fred."
Left, left and then to the right
The bombs are away and we are holding tight.
We then dive down, several hundred feet,
Out of the searchlights, that's a treat.
Back on course and homeward bound ,
"Look, there's the runway", we're down on the ground.
Off with our kit, and then for de-briefing.
Breakfast smells good, we shall soon be eating.

Roy and Irene Lingham

DECEMBER 2001

Roy and Rene slipped quietly out of Sheffield Park at the beginning of November and have gone to live in Newick. We wish them a happy and fulfilling retirement in their new home. Sheffield Park and Fletching will be very strange without them, but Roy has assured me that they won't really leave and will constantly be turning up – in fact they have already come back to the Coffee Morning and the Remembrance Service and I know he hasn't left the unofficial Footpath Group which still meets occasionally. I'm so glad that Roy gave us his reminiscences to reproduce in this magazine and I think we have some more poems for future issues! They are also continuing to take this magazine, so Good Luck and Best Wishes to you both from us all!

Mary Butterfield [Editor]

Letter from Roy Lingham

JANUARY 2002

Leaving Vigoes Farm was for all of us a very sad day, but things change, I am sure not for the better sometimes.

Seventy Nine years I have lived in Fletching Parish and, had my parents been alive, they would have been here Eighty One years. Truthfully they are still here, watching over us from the Church in Fletching, and maybe we shall join them there one day.

What was so strange to us was the quietness, after all the Cows and Calves had gone. You see, they were like a family to us; each one we reared from birth, so we knew them so well, each one an individual, knowing how some liked more Cake, Oats or Maize than their mates. They knew their own places in the Cow Shed, whether it was in the first, second or third sitting to be milked.

Still, we are not too far away, so must look on the bright side, with the New Year just beginning. Before I close, I would very much like to thank all the people that wished us well in the near future, and especially those who have thanked me for my little stories in the Mag.

16.4.2002

It is the Sixteenth of April Two Thousand and Two.

We look out of our Bedroom Window, to see the view;

The mist fills the valley, but the Church Spire pokes through.

We smile at each other, for there's lots to do,

Because Fifty Five years ago, to this very day,

Irene and Roy tied the knot, in a romantic way.

A new life for us is just abounding

From this House of strange surrounding.

No Fields or Woods are very close to us,

But just down the road you can catch a Bus.

No cows or calves, that used to give morning call;

Only cars and lorries, big and small.

But so lucky we are, to have such a wonderful sight

Of Fletching Church, by day, or by night.

Roy Lingham [Newick]

A.J. Sandells

MAY 2004

Known to most people as Jack, Mr. Sandalls was born at Sheffield Park, his Father being the Estate's Farm Foreman. He went to Fletching School until he was fourteen, the he too started working for the Estate under Mr. Tremlet, the Agent. Moving on, he went to work for Mr. Percy Mepham of Ketches Farm; there he learned to drive both tractors and cars and, because it was War time, he did not have to pass a driving test to get a licence. Next, when Mr. Cyril Griffith took over the Blacksmith at Splaynes Green, Jack did a three-month course in horse-shoeing and welding, staying at the Splaynes Green Works until he retired. He had worked there forty-four years.

He loved cricket and playing for Fletching for many years; he also helped with the Football and Darts teams. During the War he served three years with the local Home Guard.

Jack was married to Queenie for fifty-four years; they had two sons and two daughters and ten grandchildren.

Jack Sandalls died on the 4th March after a long illness. His funeral took place at Holy Cross church, Uckfield. He was cremated.

Fletching School Reunion

JULY 2004

It was on Wednesday, 19th May 2004 that the Village of Fletching came alive once again, with many faces and voices of the people that knew Fletching from the past, when it really was a Village, with two Locals, the Post Office, the Grocers and Drapers, the Bakery, Coal Merchants, Tailors, Snobs (Boot & Shoe Repairs) and the Doctor's Surgery. Of course the Butcher is still there, but the shop has moved to the other side of the House. We all met at the Rose and Crown and had lots to talk about, asking of old Friends that could not make it and of those who have sadly passed away.

There was a wonderful collection of photos from the past, in the Village Hall, put on show by Barry and Geoff. Many thanks to both of them for the hard work they have done, making such a grand collection for the future of Fletching. We all gathered in the School playground for a group photo by the local papers, and then, by kind permission of Miss Dale, the Headmistress, we toured the School, meeting the other teachers and many of the children. One thing that was missing this year was the short service that Bruce * usually conducts; but he did have a Burma Star Reunion to attend.

Once again, many thanks to Dudley for getting us all together, and may next year be as happy as this one.

* Revd Bruce Hayllar

Ernie Sandalls

AUGUST 2004

I'm sorry to say that, on the last day of June this year, Ernie Sandalls passed away after a short illness. Ernie was the elder brother of Jack, Ted and Ron, and all four boys went to Fletching School. On leaving, they all went to work on the Sheffield Park Estate, just like their father.

Ernie was given the job of helping Mr. Harry Tester, who lived in the bottom lodge. Their job was to maintain the water supply to the estate by looking after the turbine at the saw mills, close to the railway station. The reservoir was at the top of Fletching street, where the water was gravity-fed to the Mansion and the Home Farm.

It was not until the war began, when the Army took over the Park, that mains water was piped up to the reservoir from Chailey. A few years after the war the whole system was reversed, now coming from Wych Cross.

Ernie was called up as soon as war broke out and served in the army, with the Eighth. After being demobbed it was not long before he married Betty, and went to live in East Grinstead, then joining the Post Office; he worked there until he retired.

His funeral was held in Dormansland, followed by a cremation at Worth.

Fletching School Reunion, May 18th 2005

JULY 2005

Another year has passed by and once again we were blessed with a nice sunny day. Dudley Martin certainly knows how to pick them.

My first stop was the Rose and Crown, and as I walked through the door someone said, "here comes Tiddler" and looking around there were so many faces, I certainly had to put on my thinking cap to put names to them; still, after collecting my name badge, I was soon shaking hands with loads of friends and asking about those who were unable to make it this year. Sadly, there were some that were no longer with us, but definitely not forgotten.

Thanks to Barry and Geoff, the collection of Photos etc. in the Hall has improved immensely. It must be one of the best in any Sussex Village.

Then going on to visit the School for Photos and a short prayer, and thanks to Michael * for a few words, remembering those lost in the War. Looking around the School we were all impressed with the new alterations and the good behaviour of the Children, but sorry that we were losing the Head Mistress and one of her staff at the end of term.

Do hope we will all meet again next year.

* Michael Butcher

Fletching School Reunion

JULY 2006

Another year has passed by, they seem to go quicker every time we meet.

As usual we all met at the Rose & Crown, but sadly there were a few Friends that could not make it, through illness, and those that have left this earthly life for a better world.

On the way to the School, some of us visited the Village Hall to see the display of memorabilia, provided by Geoff and Barry, which was well worth a visit. On arriving at the School we were met by the Head Mistress and Staff, then group photos by the local Press, and a short service by Bruce. I can only remember once he missed, that was because he had a Burma Star Reunion in Yorkshire.

Then into the School for Tea and Biscuits and Entertainment by the Children. Once again we all thanked the Head Mistress and Dudley for all the hard work they do, getting us all together. There was a collection for the School as we all went our different ways.

Sixty Years

APRIL 2007

It was Wednesday, the Sixteenth of April, Nineteen Forty Seven, on a beautiful sunny afternoon, that Roy stood waiting in Fletching Church for Irene to come walking down the Aisle with her Father.

She was late, fifteen minutes to be correct, all because a Steam Roller decided to turn around in the road at Splaynes Green.

Many people in the Village wondered why we wanted to be married mid-week. Two reasons: first: so that Roy would not let the Football Team down on Saturday; secondly, so that his Uncle could play the Organ. Mind you, Ernie Moore * was quite agreeable if he still got his fee (7/6).

P S. I scored five goals that Saturday, costing Fred Gladman a crate of Brown Ale.

Roy and Irene Lingham

* The regular organist

Forget-me-Nots

Rene and Roy Lingham's Diamond Wedding was celebrated, as was fitting, over several days. For the Forget-me-Nots they were in fine form, their zest for partying well evident! Gwen made and decorated a delicious cake with all its trimmings; it was a fine centrepiece to our table loaded with tempting goodies.

Roy started the party with his memories of their wedding day and scoring 5 goals to win a crate of beer (bottles in those days, not cans). Rene told us about her wedding dress, made from parachute silk, and regretted she can no longer get into it. The day must have been beautiful with all the families present, as they were for the Diamond celebrations, the only difference being that Roy couldn't get a team together for football!

Una Whitehead played the piano for us all the jolly old songs for us to sing. Rene and Roy chose some of them, and if we could have jumped up and danced we would! We continued with memories of our youth (some not for your delicate ears!): the miles we walked to school; the cleaning of the homes; Zeba and Gumption; carrying water from a well or pump; brushing the carpets and giving them a good beating outside; heating the copper for the washing and baths; walking to dances, wearing dresses made on the family Singer sewing machine.

So many of the Forget-me-Nots have known each other all their lives and have shared the fun and sadness of village life, always being there for each other. Some of the men were evacuees who fell in love with the countryside and local girls and became part of the community.

Heather told me later how very much she had enjoyed hearing all the stories of Fletching as it was, with such strong, caring, hard-working (and playing) people.

Roy and Rene's son, Derek, and daughter-in-law, Ann, joined us for a very good tea and more reminiscences. How life has changed - certainly no need for the Gym in those days, or of diets - our food was all local and the vegetables and fruit grown in our own gardens. Having said that, we all remembered the day of the BANANA (after the War) - history to youngsters, but to us our youth.

Again, congratulations to Roy and Rene and their family and thanks for letting us be part of their celebrations.

Vera Cragg

Roy and Irene's Forget me Nots Golden Wedding Party

Changes

There I was just a few days ago, sitting on a wooden seat, leaning on my old Thumb Stick with JET lying at my feet, with the wind and rain doing their worst. Casting an eye forward, what is there to see? Nothing else but wire fences around the Triangle and higher ones around two thirds of Lord Sheffield's Cricket Ground. The Band Stand and Pavilion all gone.

You see, I was born the day before Empire Day 1922, and lived at Woolpack Farm until we moved to Vigoes Farm in March 1934. There I stayed until November 2001 before moving to Newick. I am still a Fletching person, always at East Park Farm, the Forget-me-Nots and the Church, where my parents are.

Living as tenants on both large Estates (Searles and Sheffield Park) I have seen so many changes in the Parish and so many stories.

Family

I shall be looking forward to next month's School Reunion, not only to meet up with old friends, but to hear and see what surprise the children have for us. You know, I get lost in this computer world, but I have no complaints of how the school is run; my Children and Grandchildren all had a first class start in life.

Our two Boys are Farmers, our Daughter with Nationwide Building Society. Six grandchildren, three Boys, three Girls: Marie did very well at Plumpton; Jason six years in the Army, including the Gulf War, now back into Farming; Ben with Virgin; * Gemma a Staff Nurse at Great Ormond Street; Rebecca who is now at the NFU office in Uckfield and Matthew is a Sergeant Crewman in the RAF, flying in Puma Helicopters. He has done three tours in Iraq, his last was a little worrying, as he was brought home, after being involved where two SAS died.

He is expecting to go back to Iraq shortly if he has not already gone. Last Summer he enjoyed flying over a few Agricultural Shows, dropping off the Paragliding Teams, and we were very glad to see him in Nov 2006 when he landed at East Park Farm for a short time, then giving us a buzz as he took off, straight over the Village Hall to wake us Forget-me-Nots up!

* Virgin Airways

The Bridge

APRIL 2008

This is a Bridge, where no water passes

And the gentle breeze waves the grasses.

This is a Bridge, with no road going through

But for us, life is good with lots to do.

This is a Bridge, that has never seen a train

For us it is a life all over, again and again

Because this is a Bridge, built ever so strong

This being Roy and Irene's true love song

Three children they had, a girl and two boys,

Who have now grown up, and passed on their toys

To the Grandchildren now, who are growing up fast

So build your Bridges strong, so that your LOVE will last.

Woolpack Farm

JUNE 2008

I stopped outside Woolpack Farm a few days ago, and thought how things have changed since I lived there. My Father and his Brother took over the tenancy in 1921 from a Mr. Langridge, and were there until 1942.

There was a large barn for the Wagons, Carts etc. Pigsties at the end of the main building which had double doors each side so that a horse could pull a wagon right through to unload. We had Cows one side and Horses the other and above them we stored our Grain. To the right there were loose boxes and a double shed that held more Cows one side and Workshop and Feed Store the other: behind them was where the Hay and Corn Stacks were built, plus piles of Mangolds, Swedes and Potatoes. Between that and the road was a large Pond where we had to pump water to the tanks in the yard. The Farmhouse had its own well for drinking water which was forty five feet deep.

There was also another large barn, hovel and yard, plus a pond, in the field on the opposite side of the road and lane. The lane used to be known as a smugglers' track leading to Ashdown Forest from the River Ouse through Sheffield Forest.

The Milk was taken daily by horse and Van to the Mid-Sussex Creamery at Sheffield Park, then put on rail to London and the South Coast. It had to be at the Dairy by 8.00 am in the Winter, Summer time 8.00 am and 4.45 pm. In 1927 Father got his first tractor and a Ford Model T lorry and began taking neighbouring Farmers' Milk.

Donald Lingham (Roy's father) at Woolpack Farm 1925

Fletching School Reunion - 21st May 2008

JULY 2008

It was Wednesday 21st of May, a bright and sunny day, just right for another School Reunion. It was a very good turnout and I think we were all so glad that we were meeting again in our old stomping ground, the Rose and Crown.

Geoff was in the Village Hall with the very fine display of photos that he and Barry have put together over the years; it was well worth a visit, it puts the Parish of Fletching well on the map.

We all arrived, or should have done, at the school by 11.00 hrs. to be welcomed by the Head Teacher, and have a group photo taken by the three local Papers. Then as usual Bruce conducted a small service, and our own Vicar, Heather, smiled with approval.

The children of classes one, two and three entertained us in their own individual way, which I am sure we all enjoyed. After that we had tea and biscuits, then a visit upstairs to the New Library, which was not there in our day.

We would like to thank the Head Teacher and her Staff once again for welcoming us all, and most of all many thanks to Dudley who spends so much of his time in getting us all together.

Memories

By the time you read this little note in the Parish Mag, the Annual School Reunion will have taken place. Sadly, there will be a few absent friends, I am sure Dudley and myself, plus our team mates, will miss the company of Ernest (Bristle) Barker our best Wicket and Goal Keeper, I always thought he was one of the best Fletching ever had, so did my dad who played for both, in the twenties.

I know we talk about the old days (well, we usually do) when we were young well before the Second World War, when Fletching Mill was working and we had one bus through the village about ten to nine a.m. and back again just before ten o'clock at night. The two Fireworks and Tea Parties Mrs. Soames gave us on the Cricket Ground in Sheffield Park, one for King George & Queen Mary's Jubilee, and Edward VIII's Accession. We had most things then in the Village: a Bakers, Butchers, Grocers, Post Office, Blacksmith, Snobs, Tailors, Doctor, not to mention Mr. Mead the Policeman, and much more I could say.

2009 Fletching School Reunion

Once again we were blessed with a warm sunny day for the Fletching School Reunion, I don't know how Dudley manages to get it right every year. We all seemed very glad to be back at the Rose & Crown before going to the School, maybe it was the Wine, Beer and good Food we had.

First we all got together on the front steps for a photo and then some more were taken around the Maypole; then as Bruce was unable to make it this year, Heather kindly took over and spoke welcoming words, followed by a short service of thanks, added to by Michael, remembering all our past Friends who did not make it back from the two great wars.

Bill then gave his usual short speech and presented the Head Teacher with a little gift, entertainment was next by the Children, followed by Biscuits and Tea and chatting about the teachers in our day, not forgetting the little cane kept for bad behaviour.

We then had a small collection for the School, and saying thanks to Maureen and all her Staff, not forgetting Geoff and all his photos, then there were many thanks to Dudley who captains the ship (unpaid). We all left with God's will, hoping to see each other again next year.

Since we held our reunion we have heard of the sad loss of Bruce Hayllar. He attended our reunions every year since they first began, with only one exception when he went to London for a Burma reunion. He and Diana also came regularly to the Foot Clinic run by the Forget-me-nots. We shall miss Bruce very much and send our deepest sympathy to Diana.

Roy Lingham goes Back in Time once again

NOVEMBER 2009

It was on Friday afternoon, the second of October, that I walked out of Fletching Church into bright sunshine, after the service for Bett Sargent, and met several people that I had not seen for some time.

David and Pat Siggs, Mick and Beryl Browne - they all sang in the Choir a few years ago, then I shook hands with Richard Hayllar and his wife, and we both spoke about being married here Sixty Two years ago, and many others.

The time was getting on so I walked under the Yew Trees to have a look at my Dad and Mum's stone, brush off the leaves so that I could read their names again, looked at the stone next to them with no name. Yes, Irene's and mine will be there one day; now I am just standing there going back in time.

No Cows next door at Church Farm, they are all down at White Barn, and there are a few of us boys walking back from Piltdown. We had walked to Uckfield to go to the Pictures, a penny's worth of broken biscuits from Woolworths and a bus ride back, all for six pennies, stopped and had a look at Mr. Joyice's Village in a Village, on to the Rec., no more old Wooden Pavilion - it burnt down. I know in the winter there used to be a very large puddle of water just outside the door, after a muddy game we would wash our knees and boots before putting on our old service greatcoats and biking home. Yes, and the School is so different, no more Saturday Night dances held there, and the Vicarage has moved, yes that's where Irene and I went to see the Vicar about having the Banns called in church. I can remember it well because Betty Bradford let us in by the Front door.

Now to go under the arch back to East Park Farm, but before I do, another look up the Fletching Street, not a car in sight, just a few people walking about, a horse and cart outside the Butcher's, it might be Mr. Alf Grover's. And yes, there's a lady coming out from the Griffin yard with a sack of coal in an old pram, and Mr. Moore just getting his bike to deliver the Letters and papers to the outlying Farms and Cottages and take their grocery orders for next week.

Wake up Roy, stop dreaming of the past.

Home Guard Christmas Dinner

DECEMBER 2009

Looking through some very old photos I found a few of Woolpack Farm, when I lived there in the twenties and early thirties. It certainly has changed, no pond beside the road, where I used to pump water into the tanks in the yard, and many changes in the buildings.

Now here is a good one, The Home Guard Christmas Dinner (1942) in the Sheffield Arms, given to us by the landlords, Mr and Mrs. Harry Grace. It was a jolly good Rabbit Stew all caught by the local poacher, and the Fruit provided for the Christmas Pudding by the Canadian Army Cookies (PLUS A FEW PINTS) it was a jolly good evening; good job Jerry was quiet.

Taking a good look at the photo I thought, yes, I am sure I can remember all those faces, most were farm and timber-yard workers.

The photo was taken by Private Reeves whose Wife had the Shop at Splaynes Green, which was once a pub or an ale house, now a private house. I am sure we were a little bit like 'Dad's Army' on the TV. There are quite a lot of stories that could be told but sadly we are very few in number now.

Sheffield Forest

MARCH 2010

I left the car at the end of East Park drive to walk up the street to post a few letters. On returning I met two lady hikers. "Is this the Footpath to get us to Trading Boundaries?" "No" said I "this is a private drive, the path you want is at the top end of the street on the left opposite the farm".

Then one lady said, "Are you a native of this area?" "Yes" said I. Then the other lady said, "Not so long ago we walked from the Nutley Arms through Sheffield Forest to what used to be The Sheffield Arms, but we did not find the ruins of a little shop in the middle of the forest we were told about. Is it true, or just another old locals' tale?"

No, it is true, there was a small house, but a little bit before my time. I know where it stood, because in my early days the outer walls were still standing and also a few rafters left; it was nearly hidden amongst the bushes. It is said that the lady that lived there made her own sweets to sell, and that she hid her money, Gold Sovereigns, in the rocks nearby. As young lads we had spent a great deal of time hunting amongst the rocks, but we did not have any luck (that's possibly an old wives' tale).

In the twenties and thirties on a Sunday afternoon and evening, parents used to bring their children for walks or picnics in the little field in the middle of the forest or beside the lake, which in those days covered nearly nine acres. There was also a boathouse with a rowing boat and a punt.

All the paths seemed to meet close to the lake, spreading out into the forest; most finished up not too far away from a pub so that

Dad & Mum could have a Beer and the children a packet of Crisps and a ginger beer.

Sheffield Forest was not the same after the Sheffield Estate was sold in 1954. All the big Oaks, Ash and Beech trees were felled and the cord wood turned into charcoal. Then the Forestry took over, killing off all the undergrowth and replanting with a variety of conifers.

Time marches on.

More memories of Woolpack Farm

APRIL 2010

Eighty eight years ago, come next month, my first visit to Woolpack Farm (two months before time) my parents had taken the tenancy from a Mr. Langridge earlier in that year.

What a lot of changes have happened to that Farm since. It was very lucky in 1940, Jerry unloaded a great deal of incendiary bombs, two falling through the roof of the Farmhouse, one burst in flames off the Landing and the other on the stone Kitchen floor. They were quickly put out with sand, as several buckets of sand were kept in the house. Others fell in the yard and some between the hay and corn stacks, but most fell in the wood opposite the Farm (no longer there).

We had no mains water. There was a pond between the buildings and the road from which water had to be pumped by hand to fill the tanks in the yard for the animals to drink. Water for the house had to be got from the well, which was forty five feet deep. When I was about eight years old my Father took me to the bottom of the well and looking up to the top it was quite frightening, as the opening looked very small. In a very dry summer we had to fetch water from a small stream.

The old Sussex barn that is now a dwelling used to house milking cows at one end and the horses at the other. When the big double doors at each side were open you could get a cart or wagon in there so that sacks of corn and potatoes could be kept in the loft.

Joined on at the south side were four pigsties and at other, at right angles, were loose boxes, also a food store and workshop, plus another cowshed for ten cows.

On the other side of the road in the first field beyond the wood was another Barn, Yard, and Hovel, also a small pond, filled in now and the building gone. A few fields further over there was a large water spring. Searles Estate had it fenced in, it had a water ramp to pump water to Searles big House - all knocked down after the second war.

So much has changed in my short time.

A very young Roy helping his father and uncle on the lorry at Woolpack Farm in 1929

Mr Bill Howe

DECEMBER 2010

I was sitting beside the Editor at Mr. Howe's birthday party and listening to his life story so far. When his daughter got to 1948, the year he became the Agent for Sheffield Park Estate, she forgot to mention that it was one of his very best challenges.

The Estate was greatly run down, not only because of the war years, but also the Tenants not seeing very much of the previous Agent, mostly on Ladyday and Michaelmas when we went to the Estate Office to pay our rent.

The very first thing that Bill did was to walk to all the Farms and meet the Tenants, look at the Land, House, Cottages and Buildings and make a note of what ought to be done to put things in good repair.

On his first visit to Vigoes, yes the Land was well farmed, the House was OK, but the Cottages needed roof repairs, also new windows and frames. Lots more could be told, perhaps another time.

School Holidays

Well here we go, the children are on their summer holidays, schools are closed until September and maybe their parents have taken them to other places, or even abroad. I know my great grandson is having a fortnight at a holiday camp and he did ask "Where did you go in your school hols?"

I shall have to think hard about this as it is my Eighty Ninth summer. At first, until I was old enough to handle a rake or a prong, I would play with other children, or sit and watch my parents and other workers in the hay and corn fields or maybe see them hoeing up and down the rows of swedes and mangolds, also potatoes. I do remember one August bank holiday in 1929 my Mother and Mrs. Isard took Grace Allan and myself to Sheffield Park Station to catch a train to Brighton - we were going to see the sea.

We were all excited and started to jump up and down on the seats to look out of the windows. Mother very sharply said "sit down or the guard will put you off the train". It was a day we never forgot. We went on a Tram to the sea front, sat on the beach with lots of other people. Then, after we had eaten our sandwiches, off came the shoes and socks, we were able to paddle in the sea.

We were very tired when we got off the train and had to walk home to Woolpack Farm. We took a short cut up through the carriage drive: this was the drive that started at what is now Archers Cottage, and came out at Holmesdale. This was the private drive used by the owners of Searles Estate, the MARYON WILSONs. As I got older there were more adventures...

School holidays

(Continued from last month)

Now that I was a little older, my Father said, "come next Monday I will take you with me to Lewes Cattle Market". That day could not come quick enough. For the market we took all the empty Milk Churns from the Lorry, put up the Sides and loaded ten Shuts in the front, and then four calves, leaving room for two more calves from Holmesdale and three from Flitteridge. Then on we went to Lewes; mind you, we had to stop at Cooksbridge to let the train go by. That was another thing I had never seen.

We arrived in the market: more Lorries, a few horse-and-carts, lots of people and drovers with long sticks herding the sheep, pigs, calves, and bullocks into their right pens, so as the buyers could have a good look at them before Mr. Wright put them under the hammer. The noise was deafening. Cattle mooing, Sheep baa-ing, Pigs squealing and everyone talking at once, Farmers having a good old chin-wag about the prices, weather, ideas old and new.

As time went by most of the stock was sold. Some of the animals were taken away by rail, which meant loading them onto cattle trucks which were then coupled up to passenger trains, to go to their new home. Dad never said anything about those the Butchers had bought.

There was in those days a lot of Cattle Markets in Sussex. I was able to visit most in future days. East Grinstead, Steyning, Heathfield, Haywards Heath, Chichester, and sometimes Guildford and Ashford.

All gone now - the only one in Sussex is Hailsham and that is in the balance, wanted by Supermarkets.

Farming is not like it used to be, not an acre of Land was wasted during World War Two. There are far too many things you cannot do now, too much interference from Government, Wildlife, Health & Safety and lots of other busy bodies.

Life on the Farm

Had a chat with Edie (that is the late Edie Moore née Appleby) at the Forget-me-Nots not so long ago about what us kids were expected to do on the Farm.

When small we could feed the Hens, collect the eggs, bottle feed the lambs and other little jobs, but as we got older jobs got harder. Spring time the sowing of the Mangolds and Swedes in rows wide enough for the Horse to walk between without treading on the plants. We had to help with the setting out of the plants with a hoe, leaving a single plant every 6 or 7 inches apart.

Then, come haymaking time, after the two Horses and Mower had cut the field for a few rounds, the outside of it was left unmown. This meant that the mower had to be turned around to go the opposite way, to cut the outside of the field. We had to hand rake the first cut of grass back just a little way so that it did not get in the way. A six acre field is a long way round for little boys. Anyone can make Hay when the sun shines, it takes a good man when it rains, shaking it all about with a prong and rake. So easy with today's equipment.

Next, the beginning of corn-cutting meant that someone with a scythe mowed about a six foot space around the field, and that corn had to be bundled up to make a sheaf and tied up with a bond made out of several strands of straw, then laid to one side until after all the field was cut, and we stacked all the sheaves into piles of six or eight. Then came the building of ricks, thatching and finally thrashing, we always got the dirty job of caval raking, another job done today all in one go by - THE COMBINE HARVESTER.

By now it was nearly time to go potato picking, and pulling up the mangolds and swedes, carting them off near to home, making a long pile, covering them up with bracken first, then earth.

Life on the Farms can be very lonely with one person doing most jobs on his own, not like the company we all had, no banter between different Farmworkers in the Local.

Water Works

We have all seen the workmen who come either to dig up, or fill a pothole in the road, how before they start have to take their road signs up and down the road, to warn the traffic of long delays. Well, something came to mind from just talking to a friend I have made since moving to Newick. In our conversation I happened to mention that Mr. Howe would be one hundred and one at the end of October. "Do you know him?" was the reply, "my father used to do a lot of work for the Sheffield Park Estate years ago, mostly plumbing." "Then he must have been Mr. Fuller," said I. "Yes" was the reply. Now this brings me back to the first bit of my story.

The Estate's water used to be pumped up from the River Ouse close to the Sheffield Park Railway Station to the underground reservoir at the top of Fletching street, where it was gravity-fed through filters to the big house and Estate Office, Farm Buildings, Walkwood and Vigoes Farm.

In the late 1930s the new tenant who took over Pound Farm asked for water to be laid on for his animals and House. This meant crossing the main road, A275. I was very interested in this as Mr. Fuller did not dig up the road, but dug his trench from Vigoes Building to the edge of the road, and on the opposite side dug his trench to Pound Farm. Then with some sort of ratchet machine he forced the ¾ inch pipe with a point on the front right under the road into the trench on the other side (no traffic delays). The only thing was, as the water pressure was low, when our cows were drinking no water got to Pound Farm.

It was later on when the Canadian Troops were stationed in

Sheffield Park, they laid mains water on from Chailey.It was in the late Fifties that it all changed and our mains water came from the Reservoir at Wych Cross.

Blue Sapphire Wedding Anniversary

APRIL 2012

CONGRATULATIONS to Roy and Irene Lingham, who were married 65 years ago, on 16th April, 1947. We wish them both good health and many more years of happiness together.

Editors

It was the sixteenth of April 1947, a very bright sunny afternoon, the Church clock had just struck 2, and the Bells were quiet. The organist had nearly finished playing the Wedding March, but that was not Ernie (Mr. Moore) at the organ, it was my Uncle. I had a few weeks earlier agreed to pay Ernie his Seven and Sixpence fee!

Well there were Irene and I standing together, with the Reverend Burns-Cox towering over us saying, in rather a loud voice, "We are gathered here this afternoon to marry this man and woman…" etc. That certainly seems a very long time ago and so much has changed in the Parish of Fletching: the two big estates sold up, no Bakers, Butchers, Post Office, Village Policeman or Doctor. Only two farms left that have dairy cows; one time of day I used to collect milk from fifteen farms in the Parish. Happy days.

The Thirties

One morning not so long ago I was walking through the Park* with Ann (my daughter-in-law) and Jet their dog to feed the Ducks on the Lower Lady Lake, also to check the cattle in the pipe field, so named because the old sewage pipe runs just above the ground at a few places. Going past the Cricket Ground I began to think of memories I had of that place, going back to the thirties when it was King George V and Queen Mary's Jubilee.

Mrs. Soames opened the cricket ground for a Sports Day with a Tea, Band, and Fireworks in the evening, also for us children a medal and a cup. She did the same thing when Prince Edward became King for the Coronation which never happened! I still have both Medals and cups!

The old Pavilion, which had a spiral stairway up to the second floor, was to us boys something we enjoyed climbing, and some week-ends when the grounds were open to the public Mrs. Edwards, who was the Landlady of The Sheffield Arms, used to serve teas there. To my way of thinking, Lord Sheffield had built it in a perfect place, not seen from the big house but the pitch in full view, unlike where the new pavilion is today - looking right into the afternoon sun.

When the War started and the MOD took over the Park it was not very long before the Nissen Huts were erected in the woods around the grounds. Some of the footings are still to be found there after all this time. First there were British troops, then Canadians, and the Cricket Ground was let go, with tanks and other armoured cars running all over it. When Mr. Howe became the Estate Manager he very soon had the ground cleared, ploughed and sown with buckwheat for the pheasants. After the estate was sold it took a lot of time to get it back to its present state.

* Sheffield Park

Land Girls

Watching Land Girls on TV and in films you would think they had a glamorous life, but it was so different in those hard times. Sadly the three Land Army Girls that lived in the Parish that I knew very well have passed on to a better world (MAYBE) - there was Ivy Funnel, Gladys Setford and Winnie Padgam.

Win used to be with three other girls travelling around the farms with the Thresher and Steam Engine. They took it in turns: two on the corn stack with pitchforks (or prongs) passing the sheaves of Barley, Wheat or Oats on to the machine where the other two girls were, one cutting the strings of the sheaves while the other one fed them into the Threshing machine and it had to be evenly done, because if they let a whole one go through it made the Steam Engine cough a little and the Driver make a rude remark. It was not an easy job with all the dirt and dust especially when the young ladies first started with their hands being quite soft. I have seen some with bleeding blisters. You know, some of the very old Farmers did not think the girls could do a man's work, but were very soon proved wrong.

Those L.A.G.s who had to learn to milk the cows, most were a little nervous at first, the cows knew it and some kicked out, and to have a horse tread on your foot or an old sow with a young litter come for you when you went to clean her Pigsty - life for them was not very pleasant, looking back at some of the very cold, wet and frosty winters.

Many of the girls lodged in a very large house at the top of Cinder Hill close to Newick and had to cycle to work very early in the morning. There were two Fashion Models, Kay and Eileen, who had joined the L.A. staying at the Sheffield Arms: one to help in the Market Garden which was the Tennis Court and Bowling Green which had to be dug up (but spent most of her time behind the bar); the other one was with the Countess at Sliders Farm.

Parish Magazines

The other day I thought, what's in that old box under the stairs, shall I have a look? No, it will only make more work, but being nosy I just had to have a look. There was quite a lot of Books, Mags and Photos and a tied up bundle of Fletching Parish Magazines which I remember was loaned to Sussex University when they came to interview me, and make some recordings on tape of what Farming was like before the War II in and around the Parish.

Looking back through these Mags just to see what I had written in them several years ago. In one printed in April 2001 was an article about the Fletching Home Guards' Christmas Dinner in the Sheffield Arms 1943, also a good photo of us sitting at the tables, taken by Private Reeve who used to live at the small shop at Splaynes Green, now a private house; I think that in early days it was a Pub or Ale House where some of the local poachers traded goods for beer.

Looking very hard at this Photo I was able to name everyone there, but don't think there are many of us left.

It was in May 1940 that the call came for volunteers to join the LDV (Local Defence Volunteers) to help in the defence of our country, so most of the men and youths of the Parish stepped forward. After a few weeks things got a little bit better organised and we became the Home Guard attached to the 17th Battalion Royal Sussex D Company, our Platoon was under Capt. Tremlet who was also the Agent for Sheffield Park Estate.

Before we did any training the first thing was to have about six persons a night to watch out for Paratroops and ask walkers for their Identity Card. One night while on duty 10 - 12, Jack Sandalls and myself heard some people coming. Halt, who goes there? said Jack. Instead of stopping, three ladies came straight at us. You know who we are, said Mrs. Richardson, you stupid boys. With her were Ada Setford and Julia Wilkens, coming back from a Red Cross meeting. So much for Dad's Army! And the first weapons we had to stop Jerry was one Ross Rifle, twelve shotguns and a box of Petrol Bombs.

Four generations of Linghams

L. to r: Roy Pendennis, Lois (nee Ashdown) Donald Pendennis,

Derek Pendennis

Fletching Football Team (Roy in centre)

Dungspreaders Ball 1935

(Roy in cap)

Roy with Derek on Jimmy Edwards' donkey

Fletching School Reunion 2009

L to R Michael Butcher, Roy Lingham, Peter Richardson

Pals meeting in the Rose and Crown prior to School Reunion

Roy Lingham

FEBRUARY 2013

We were very sorry to learn that Roy had broken his hip and has been in the Princess Royal undergoing repair!

He is now in Meadow Lodge Rehab. Unit in Lewes and we send him every good wish for a speedy return home.

Editors

The train to East Grinstead

APRIL 2013

Firstly, I would very much like to thank all those who sent me Christmas and get well Cards; it is nice to know that you are still thought of while in Hospital. And many thanks to those who came to cheer me up. I'm now going to write a few more lines about old times.

I am told that at last the Bluebell Railway has broken through to East Grinstead. I do hope that I shall be able to make that journey once more; it will bring back so many memories of schooldays. There used to be six of us from the Village that travelled daily.

Mary Burns, who lived in a Keeper's Cottage down Sheffield Mill Lane; Frank Edwards, whose parents were the landlords of the Sheffield Arms, now Trading Boundaries; Jack Pickwell, whose father was the chauffeur for Mrs. Soames and lived in one of the Flats beside Sheffield House, as we called it; next, Roger Mepham, whose parents worked and lived at Flitteridge Farm. And there were two likely lads from the Village: David Claridge whose Mum & Dad ran the shop and Post Office, and moving up the street to The Griffin was Mr. & Mrs. Bently's son Steve; his dad was very much involved with the Cricket and Football teams.

We all arrived at Sheffield Park Station to catch the early train, taking good care to behave when Mr. Perkins (Station Master) was about. More boys and girls joined us at Horsted Keynes, West Hoathly, Kingscote and then we had to walk from East Grinstead Station to the County School at Windmill Lane.

We did not all come home on the same train, but a few of us young ones soon learned that to do our homework in the school library, then come home on a later train (6.00 pm) at Sheffield

Park, gave us more time to play - that is, if we hadn't got some odd jobs to do!

We would like extend to Roy and Irene a warm welcome home and a warm welcome back to these pages.

Editors

Bill Howe

It was back in 1948 that Mr. Howe became the new Agent for the Sheffield Park Estate and I remember one of the first things he did was to walk almost all of the Estate. I first met him when he came to visit Vigoes Farm to check it all over. With his stout staff we walked the woods and fields and the buildings, Cottages and Farm House (no book or pencil, but I did not know then what a good memory he had). Now at this sad time I will write no more, but in the future, maybe, my 65 years of knowing Uncle Bill (as I called him) will be interesting.

Bill Howe died on 2nd April 2013 aged 102.

Sheffield Park Station

MAY 2013

There are still a lot of people interested in watching and hearing the old steam trains, the shunting of trucks and switching of points when the whistle blew. We boys often spent time watching them at Sheffield Park on a Saturday morning. As a country Station it really was in those days a busy little place, being only a single track from Horsted Keynes to Colver Junction where it joined the Uckfield-Lewes line. About four times day you had an up and down train in Sheffield Park Station, 7am, 10am, 2pm, 6pm.

The Mid-Sussex Dairy and Turners Timber Yard were both joined to the goods yard and in the winter time the milk going to London and Brighton in 17 gallon churns had to be on the platform by 9.50; in Summer time the milk used to be ready for the two 6 o'clock trains. The goods train coming from Lewes had to be shunted off the main line by 9.55, then, after both passenger trains had departed, the goods train would start to push trucks into their places, one to the goods shed, coal truck to another siding, and if they had got some big trees they were taken into the timber yard then away to Horsted Keynes, West Hoathly, Kingscote and East Grinstead, returning to Sheffield Park just before 2pm.

There were three coal merchants who had truck loads of coal left there: Mr. Bentley, Fletching; Mr. Emmens, Nutley; Mr. Coates, Dane Hill. Local farmers used it quite a lot. We used to have truck loads of Keep sheep from Romney Marsh to look after for about three months. That was good fun, driving them up to Woolpack Farm via the carriage drive from Moyses to Homesdale.

Irene Kathleen Mary Hollingdale

(Rene Lingham)

AUGUST 2013

Born on a dark and stormy night
It gave my mother an awful fright
September was the month that I was due
But why I came in July I haven't a clue.

School days were fun, I had a good friend
But on the last term, it all had to end.
I went away on my very first job
Work was so hard, for just a few bob.

Becoming a Marine Wren, when War came along
Through the Blitz in Pompey, I had to be strong.
In a Bar when on leave, it was a great joy
I found a nice fellow, whose name was Roy.

It was after the War that we got wed
Using our Docketts for a table, chairs and bed.

Two Boys and a Girl are the Children we had.
Now six grandchildren, that can't be bad
They visit us often, and bring us good cheer.
As time passes by, in our twilight year.

David Siggs

January 1997

Our Postman for many years

Some mornings are cold, some are bright

We look for the Postman, if he is in sight.

Here he comes, Why it's David this week.

He has the Letters and Bills, Oh what a cheek.

But things are not that bad : he has a smile

Come in quick, and sit for a while

He has a cup of tea, and then on his way

It was his first stop, since he started this day

Then off in his Red Van, away up the road

Not many more times will he be bringing the load

Soon he will be sixty, and coming no more

How we will miss him, that is for sure.

Farming Then and Now

OCTOBER 2013

Watching Countryfile on TV I thought what a great number of changes in farming I have seen in my Ninety One years.

As a very young boy all the farms in Fletching Parish had horses to do the heavy work and most of them went to the Blacksmiths at Splaynes Green, Mr. Packham, and Sheffield Green, Mr. Nordon, to have their new shoes.

My Father had three cart horses and one Welsh Cob that pulled the cart with the 17 gallon Milk Churns to and fro the Mid-Sussex Dairy at Sheffield Park. Moving on, he later had his first Lorry, a T. Model Ford.

These Churns usually stood in the cow stall where the cows were milked by hand, bucket & stool, then the milk was tipped into the churns which had a piece of muslin over the top held by three or four clothes pegs. No strainer or collar in those days (no Health & Safety). To keep the milk cool overnight some farms stood the churns in a tank of water in the pond.

Now for harvesting and haymaking (no silaging until after the 2nd World War), grass cut, turned two or three times and built into a rick or stack weather permitting, and as soon as the stack had sunk down it had to be thatched; nowadays cut and baled in no time.

As for cutting the corn, the combine starts and the corn is taken away and straw baled or chopped finely to be ploughed in, all done in a day. In my early days one man with a scythe cut a six foot swathe around the field all being tied up by hand; that was so that the horses pulling the binder did not trample it down. Then the corn sheaves are stood up in sixes, collected, built into a stack, thatched and wait until the thrasher came, then that meant building a straw stack; that usually meant work for 7 to 8 men.

Fields of Mangels, Swedes and Kale all had to be thinned out by hand with horse and shim to keep the rows clear of weeds. When ready for pulling they were stored for the winter, then chopped up for the stock, as most farms did not have mains water, only from ponds or wells.

Moving on to some of the outside and field jobs on the farm: muck spreading, now all loaded into the spreader by tractor and front loader then taken into the fields and emptied.

What a difference in time! We used to load the dung into a horse and cart by manual labour, take it into the field and make small lumps four yards apart, then later on spread it all with long-handled forks; not quite as good as the spreaders of today.

Ploughing a field with one man, two horses and single-furrow plough, it would take him nearly a day to plough an acre. Today they just start at one side of the field using a five-furrow reversible plough; it seems to me the only time that one takes pride in ploughing is at ploughing matches.

When I started with a tractor and two-furrow plough, first you had to mark out the headland, that being about four or five yards in all around the outside of the field. Then you ploughed the inside, having to measure it in cants, finally doing the outside headland. The first time for me, when I had finished the first cant and started another, I had left a small piece of land not ploughed, about 3 to 4" and 10 yards long. So that it was not seen by someone else, I turned it over with a spade.

Hedge cutting today is done very quickly with tractor and

flail cutter and no clearing up. For us it was a winter job in between milking, feeding, hay-cutting from the rick, and bedding and watering the animals. Our hedge cutting was done with a slasher or swap and hooker, raking up and making a bonfire, sometimes in wet and cold weather. We had a "West of England" sack round our shoulders, held together by a four-inch nail. These sacks were thick and strong because they always held 2¼cwt of wheat; we thought nothing of carrying them on our back, only ½cwt allowed today.

The Woodsman

The man that thatched the Hay, Corn and Straw Stacks was also a woodsman spending most of his time in the winter out in the woods and hedges. His main job was to keep the hedges trimmed, but if one had not been cut for a few years then this was cut and relaid with heathers and stakes. The heart of this job was to know what to leave and what to cut out.

In large woods they usually cleared a cant every five years, all except the hardwood trees like oak, ash and beech. These were left for later years for timber. When cutting hazel the long straight sticks about six feet long were used for thatching by splitting them down the middle to make spars and rods. Nothing in those days was wasted, even all the rough bits were bundled up to make faggots to keep the coppers boiling.

Now that the stacks or ricks had settled down, time for the thatcher to start to keep them dry. First he would rake the roof and sides, then make a bed of wheat straw, lay something heavy on top after watering well so that he could pull out little bunches of straight straw; these were called flows. They were kept apart by putting them criss-cross one over another, carried up the ladder and gently laid one upon another, starting at the bottom of the roof and working up to the top, gently raking down then fixing the spars and rods to hold them in place. The last job was to trim all the rough edges with the clippers; that's all finished for another year. Not any more, we have moved with the times. Soon it will be all done by pressing a button.

Royal Visit

I am really digging deep into the old grey matter now, back to the mid Nineteen Thirties, when Queen Mary came to visit Mrs. Soames and walked around the garden at Sheffield Park.

Just a few things that happened on this particular day: firstly Jack Pickwell and I were playing close to the Stable and Coach House next to Sheffield House when Mr. Harry Pickwell (Mrs. Soames' chauffeur) told us not to go anywhere near the grounds and garden. Taking no notice, we wandered off but were seen by Queen Mary's guards. This meant a spanking from Jack's DAD.

Another thing that comes to mind is that next day the Queen's visit to Sheffield Park was in the daily papers and on the front page of the News Chronicle was four year old Stanley Setford opening the gates at North Lodge for the Queen's car to pass through. Mr. and Mrs. Setford lived in the Lodge before moving in to the Forge on Sheffield Common.

Stephens Farm and Wilmshurst

MARCH 2014

My mate called in for a chat the other day and said, "You lived close to Stephens Farm and Wilmshurst in the twenties and thirties. What was it like then?"

Wilmshurst was owned by a Mr. and Mrs. Wild; the gardener was Mr. Willie and the handyman Mr. Wise (the three Ws). There was a Cook and a Maid, also a 14 year-old boy, Matthew Tester, who used to come and collect milk from Woolpack Farm every morning about 6.45.

All the fields were rented out to the Lingham Bros. Here's just a few things that came to mind: One summer when the hay-making was in progress on one of the hilly fields, the carter turned the two horses too sharp and over went a wagon load of hay. Both horses were OK as the shafts broke. Another time, in the field that was nearly surrounded by Sheffield Forest, the hay had been raked up into rows, all by hand, when suddenly a whirly wind came and took most of the hay into the trees, also two little frogs. Another time that comes to mind was when my father was ploughing the field close to the drive when a fox came racing across the field, shortly followed by the hounds and then the huntsmen - over the hedge at the end of the field and so did the two horses pulling the plough - Father and all! The plough stuck in the hedge, Father in the ditch, and the two cart horses away with the Hunt, later caught at Holmesdale.

The other thing was that Mr. Wise used to like, during his time off, to take his 12 Bore Gun around the woods and fields, but when walking home he would carry the gun behind his back, one hand on the butt and the other with two fingers in the barrels.

Yes, it did, in the end, blow both fingers off.

One of the Ladies that worked in the house got married and had two daughters; the eldest married my Mate's older brother.

Stephens Farm

Stephens Farm at that time was about eighteen acres, and the lower fields where the brook runs through rather boggy.

The Farmhouse was built on the side of the track coming out of Sheffield Forest on its way to Nutley and Ashdown Forest, known as the Smugglers' track. Up to the first floor level it was blocks of stone, then timber-framed and roof, a little outdoor shed and loo. The Sussex Barn was next to the Forest. It also housed the few cows and a horse.

It belonged to the Sheffield Park Estate and was rented by Mr. and Mrs. Osborne, and he used to bring his small amount of Cows' milk in two buckets (A.M and PM) to weigh it and then empty it into the Lingham's churns, and settled up once a month. He then used to go off on his motor bike (which he kept at Woolpack Farm) to work for H & E Waters of Forest Row.

They had two children: a girl Margaret and a boy Henry; my mother helped to bring them into the world. The boy in later life took a Farm on Ashdown Forest. The Osbornes are a well-known family on the Forest, going back several years they had the Foresters' Arms at Fairwarp and a daughter was married to the Landlord of The William the Fourth, now the Nutley Arms.

Henry now farms on Ashdown Forest and is well known all over the Forest and all the surrounding Villages.

Pound Farm

What do we know about Pound Farm? Firstly it had one of the first V1s to explode, in the field between the Farm House and the A275. It killed two Cart Horses but the Six Bullocks that were lying close where it landed escaped unhurt. What do we know about Winter Cottage (now Little Manor)? Windows and doors were broken in the houses close by and the curtains in Winter Cottage fell and trapped the Lady in bed. For a long time there was a small piece of metal stuck in the woodwork of Pound House.

Let's go back in time to the twenties. On the Common, opposite the Sheffield Arms, once a year a small Fair with swings etc. pitched there for one day only, and in the field next to it races were held. My Mother, with Mr. Percy Mepham of Ketches Farm, won the three-legged race. At that time the Tenant of Pound Farm was Mr. O. Wood, followed by Mr. & Mrs. Tester and their two Sons Jack and Bill. They moved in on March 29th 1934 - the same day as we moved into Vigoes Farm. My Dad and Mr. Tester, as they both had Common rights, agreed to let their cows feed on the same day so that we three boys could attend them from the cross roads to Paygate. Not much traffic in those days.

Commander Scott came for a short time, then Mr. & Mrs. Ayers who stayed several years; their son married a local Farmer's daughter and moved into Bull Cottage. In March 1954 when the Sheffield Park Estate was sold, Pound Farm had new owners.

I think Mr. O'Connor was the next owner - quite a lad - had not been married long, his wife a daughter of Grant's Whisky.

One morning he asked me to pull his car out of the ditch, mentioning that he always drove better drunk than sober! Finally his marriage broke up and new people moved in. They wanted to take down the two staircases and just have one going up from the front Door. I don't know the full story but it was to do with an inside wall. English Heritage was called in and it got moved a few inches. A few outbuildings were taken down and the fields let.

Father's Day – Dad's Army

SEPTEMBER 2014

A gift for me on Fathers' Day was a pair of socks. It had words stamped in them "Home Guard, Dad's Army". This took me back a long way, to be exact Seventy Four Years.

It was first called The Local Defence Volunteers, (L.D.V.), in which those that joined did two or three nights a week watching out for the Enemy action, at different places around the Parish and with someone on a Bike to report to the local Police (P.C. Bert Meads).

In a very short time the L.D.V. was scrapped and the Home Guard (H.G.) formed under the Ministry of Defence. We then became a Platoon in D Company, 17th Battalion, Royal Sussex Regiment, Headquarters at East Grinstead.

The Reading Room at Sheffield Green (a tin Hut built for the locals and Estate workers by the late Mrs Soames) was taken over for Equipment, Training and Night Guard. Every night of the week there used to be five Privates and one N.C.O. with an Officer in attendance. They did four shifts a night, from 10 pm - 12, 12 - 2, 2 - 4, 4 - 6 am.

At first our armament was one 303 Ross Rifle, twelve Shotguns and a few Pick Handles - not four candles! (2 Ronnies) and a Home Guard Arm Band. At that time it was thought that if Jerry turned up we might be able to hold the River and Railway Bridges and the Station. Now with afterthought NO CHANCE, but the spirit was there. I think that we could have mustered forty HGs, First World War men, farm workers, timber yard and us likely lads, all who might have registered for National Service. There were seven of us but I am the only one left. Maybe I am the last Fletching Home Guard.

Changing Rural Life

Just last week I was asked: "What do you think your house is worth at today's prices?" (don't know). Well, it is just a little above the price of the whole of the Sheffield Park Estate, sold March 1954 for £250,000.

Thinking back all those years ago my Father and I had great problems in raising the money to buy Vigoes Farm which was sold to us for £5,000, that being the Farmhouse, 2 Cottages, the Farm Buildings and just over 80 acres of Land which included 5 acres of Woodland.

At that time the Sheffield Arms (now Trading Boundaries) was on a Long Lease to Tamplins Brewers of Brighton. Just a short note: the hearsay is, when Lord Sheffield had the pub built it was called The New Inn but this was not liked by his Lordship, he preferred The Sheffield Arms. At that time the Farm went with the Hotel, as it now became a "Change Horses" on the Croydon, East Grinstead, Lewes, Brighton stage coach route. This was all finished when Lewes to East Grinstead Railway was built, then LBSR.

Things changed after the end of the 1st World War. The Farm that went with The Sheffield Arms became Vigoes Farm, named after the two Cottages that are now turned into one - Greystones. Vigoes Farmhouse was built in 1919 by Joby Luxford, now H & E Waters of Forest Row; and the Cottage that went with The Sheffield Arms now became Vigoes Cotts instead of Sheffield Arms Cottages.

Great changes have happened since I was a Boy; most of the Farms are different, no Cows to produce milk which was fresh daily for the local community. Now it's days old, not got the goodness in it like it used to be. I've drunk milk straight from the cow most of my life; now they say it's not good for you! More changes - the Farm Cottages no more: large houses, two into one, great bits added on, just different People changing Rural Life.

Roy Lingham 92 years young

The Women's Land Army Girls

NOVEMBER 2014

Someone in high places has just got round to thanking those of the Women's Land Army after all these years (bit late as usual), not too many now to hear the thanks they should have had years ago.

It was not an easy job, cold, wet and frosty in the Winter and the Summer just as bad, dusty and dirty. Most jobs were done by hand, like hoeing, pitching, muck-spreading, mangold and swede-pulling, kale-cutting. Let's not forget the miles they did, walking up and down the rows of crops, leading a horse or walking behind, holding the reins of two horses rolling, harrowing. Must not forget the milk maids; a lot of the young ladies had only seen pictures of cows, let alone milked one. Not too bad looking after calves and young stock, but to be given a bucket and stool and told to milk that cow - that's a work of art to get milk out of a cow. If she didn't like you she would not let it down and if you sat down on her wrong side she would very soon kick you over.

Some of the young ladies lived in on the Farms they worked at, but quite a good few were billeted in a large house at the top of Cinder Hill, Newick. A few that went with the traction engine and thrashing machine traveled around the different farms in a caravan towed behind. Hobdens of North Chailey had three sets of thrashing machines. I remember all the drivers, Bill Night, John Johnson and Bob Parker.

Some older farmers at first were not sure that Land Army ladies could do the job, so some would put them to difficult jobs and sit back and smile. Like at one farm two new girls arrived who were to thrash a stack of peas and tears. These, when stacked, were little loose bundles. When building a stack you always started from the outside and worked to the middle and when taking it to pieces for thrashing you took the roof off first, making sure you started from the middle and worked to the outside, layer by layer or you could lug and tear your inside out. After watching for a few minutes the engine driver told the Farmer to take those new girls down and put two old farm hands on the job. When all was finished the said Farmer asked one girl "And what are you doing to-night?" "Going to the Bull" (meaning the pub called The Bull in Newick). The Farmer laughed; he saw it in a different light.

Irene Lingham

The very first time I met Irene was on her first 48-hour pass from the Royal Marines. She had come to stay with her Auntie May who lived at Furners Green and worked at the Sheffield Arms. Jack Sandalls and I had gone in for a drink before doing an all-night guard in the Reading Room at Sheffield Green (Fletching Home Guard HQ). Her leave over, I did walk to the station with her to catch the 6 o'clock train to Brighton and then on to Portsmouth. We said we would keep in touch by letter; that was the beginning of a five- year friendship. She was demobbed early in 1946; we got engaged on 13th August 1946. Her mother thought it was a bad omen (how wrong she was, bless her!) We were married in Fletching church on 16th April 1947 at 2 p.m. Blue skies, lovely day, party at the Sheffield Arms. We left the party to catch the 6 o'clock train to Brighton, then to the flicks before catching a bus to Poynings Cross-roads. We were going to spend two days with Rene's Nan and Grandad at Clappers Lane, Fulking. It was a very long walk, so Grandad gave us a very large whisky; we both slept like a log until breakfast time!

We lived with my parents until the Estate's Decorator had put No. 2 Vigoes Cottage in order and also took up the brick floors and laid a concrete floor and the outside loo. We had dockets to buy one table, four chairs, a bed, dressing table and a single wardrobe. Relatives fitted us with pots and pans. In those days all the tradesmen called, the grocer, the butcher and baker. We had milk from the Farm. We worked 7 days a week from 5 a.m. till we finished about 8 p.m., wages Four Pounds a week.

Rene had always worked in service – she was an Officers' Steward in the Royal Marines. So she had to learn how to farm. She had plenty of teachers – Dad, Mum and me! Everybody sat down and did a bit of milking. Later on she took to driving a tractor, but she wouldn't drive the car! She did hoeing, hedge clearing (raking up after we had cut it); she worked with my mother on that.

In March 1954 Sheffield Park Estate went up for sale, that was a surprise! We all managed to pull together to buy Vigoes Farm – Five Thousand pounds. It took a few years to level out. Our stay at Vigoes lasted until October 2001; we then moved to Newick. Our children were married and had left the nest. Rene and I had five good years here before she started to go downhill with the horrible dementia. She was a wonderful wife and mother, grandmother and friend. (Irene died on the 29th December 2014)

Irene in her Easter Bonnet

The Forget-me-Nots

A Fletching Village Club for the Over Sixties. Rene and I, with Gladys Setford and Joan Kilby, joined the Club just over thirty years ago, but we have never really known how and when it first started. The tale goes that Miss Ford and Mrs. Howe were involved; perhaps it will all come to light one day.

It was just a pound for a year's subscription in those days, and that included tea (sandwiches and cakes made by our good Lady members and a cuppa in the cups and saucers decorated with forget-me-nots). That tea service I think was given to the Club by Miss Ford.

At each monthly meeting we bring a little something for a Raffle. The things that happen throughout the year are usually Valentine's Lunch, Speakers, Visitors, Garden Centre visits, Places of interest and Easter Bonnet Competition. Christmas Dinner was always at the Rose and Crown, but now we have different venues owing to the best prices we can all afford. This takes place in late November, as December is kept for the Christmas Bring-and-Buy and our own Christmas Party and Tea.

At this year's February Fish and Chip Lunch I sat beside Jack, Derek and Ann. First we each spoke about our loss and then it got round to couples that have departed from the Club whom we knew so well: Mr. and Mrs. Howe, Eddie and Edie Moore, Fred and Ada Gladman, Ron and Pauline Cash, Ron and Georgie Horscroft, also Mrs. Beech, Mrs. Morley (Lesley's Grandmother). We could go on and on – gone, but not forgotten.

Come to think about it, until Robert became Treasurer we all had no idea of the Club's finances. Now everything is in black and white and we are told once a year how we stand.

As we were getting ready to go home, Rose said to me: "You're so slow now with your walking, from when you used to be the fastest runner on the football pitch." "Yes" I said, "do you remember the lorry that took us to matches? We sat on forms in the dark under a canvas sheet." "Yes" she said. Then out of the blue she asked "What happened to Rene's brother, Ron? I didn't half fancy him." I replied "He fancied you." "He never said. I might have been your sister-in-law." That was nearly Seventy years ago.

Forget me Nots Easter Bonnet Parade

Footpaths of Fletching Parish

MAY 2015

It must have been over 30 years ago that the same problem came up at a Parish Council meeting, of which Mrs. Rumble wrote in March's magazine.

There were a few of us that took up the challenge. We formed a Footpath Committee, meeting once a month at Sharps, Piltdown. We were Sonia Harriyott, Joan Smith, Beryl Browne, Mary Butterfield, Stan Setford, myself and, taking the chair, Denis Kenward. Sonia wrote out a description of the walks and the accompanying maps were drawn by Joan Smith.

There are several nice walks to the Sloop pub, via Lane End, through Wapsbourne Wood, also Ketches Farm, Kings Wood, passing over or under the Bluebell Railway, and the River Ouse. Sheffield Forest has many interesting paths, starting from Trading Boundaries (to me it is still The Sheffield Arms). You will meet up with other paths at Sheffield Mill, from Furners Green, Colin Godmans, Wilmshurst, Moyses Farm, Northall and Woolpack Farm, the main one passing alongside the Mill Pond, known to many Oldies as The Smugglers' Track. (Now back to hearsay: small barges came up the Ouse to Sheffield Bridge, then Pack Horses through to Nutley and then on through Ashdown Forest.)

If starting at Fletching Church, paths spread out like the spokes of a wagon wheel to Moyses, Clapwater, Black Ven, Barkham and Newick. They nearly all used to end up at a pub nearby, in my day.

Donald Lingham

It was Sunday morning, 19th April, 2015, just before 6.00 a.m., that I switched on the radio, as I do every day, but on this day after the News a lady began to talk about the injured soldiers of the 1914-18 War, who wore a blue uniform.

My Father was one of them, shot right through the chest in late 1917. He was taken back to Dover after Christmas, then on a train to Victoria Station, where the soldiers were left on stretchers with a label round their necks saying which place they would be sent to next.

As they lay on the platform the man next to Dad said "Where are they sending you, mate?" "To Lancashire" was the reply. "That's my home and I've got to go somewhere in Sussex." So, after a short chat, labels were quickly changed, so my Father's next stop was at Greylingwell Hospital, Chichester, Sussex. After that he went to Sommerville Camp, Eastbourne. There they were allowed out in the afternoons, just to wander around. One time Dad and a mate walked on to the local Golf Course and lay down in a bunker out of the wind. They had not been there long before a golf ball rolled in with them. Soon, two ladies came for their ball and, seeing those two men in hospital blue, took them into an Eastbourne hotel for the afternoon. They were none other than a theatre actress, Gladys Cooper, and her sister. This happened a few more times. It was later in Dad's life that, at some place, he met Robert Morley, one of Gladys Cooper's step-sons. I have seen him in several TV films; one that comes to mind is *The Magnificent Men in their Flying Machines*, also *Cromwell.*

Sheffield Mill

JULY 2015

My stories of Sheffield Mill might be true, or might be hearsay. You see, my first visit to the Mill was on a Sunday evening walk from Woolpack Farm, with my Mum and Dad, not forgetting Rex, the farm Collie dog. We walked the so-called Smugglers' Track, which went from Northall Farm right through Sheffield Forest to Nutley, then on to Ashdown Forest. We passed by Mr. Osborne's farm building (belonging to Stephens Farm), then entered the Forest going gently down hill, with a large water spring on the right where the overflow water finally got into the Mill Pond. This was also filled by two other small streams, one from Danehill joined by the one from Colin Godmans, and another from Wilmshurst. From the little valley we climbed up the hill where the tall Beech trees grew, passed them going down through the rocks. (The tale goes that an old lady who lived in the house at the bottom and made sweets to sell, hid her gold coins there. Later in life, we boys searched high and low – no luck!). The ruins of the house were still there; it was where two paths met. We went on past the Boat House, which housed a rowing boat and a punt. The lake then covered nearly nine acres of water up to the Mill House. My Dad knew Mr. Steel, the tenant farmer, as he used to collect his two milk churns at the top of Mill Lane, Furners Green.

It is said that the first water wheel was built to work bellows, to help smelt the rocks for iron stone, which was then taken to the village of Blackboys to help make some of the first English cannons. It was later that the water wheel was used to drive the mill for corn grinding. The last Miller was Mr. Rayward who had three daughters. Two of them married two brothers, the Mepham Bros. who were tenant farmers.

Mr. Marcellow was the next tenant. Once a year he used to have a Dungspreaders Ball, helped by his London friends, Jack Jagger, Mabel, her sister Edie, and her friend Tressie. Her father owned most of the tugs on the Thames. (We were now living at Vigoes). Next came Capt. Hunt, the last tenant before the Sheffield Park Estate was sold. He bought it as a sitting tenant. He was a very remarkable character; I could write quite a story about him……

The next owner was a doctor of something, but he did not stay long. Then the new owners were Mr. and Mrs. Ingram. He was the Editor of the London Illustrated News and his wife was a writer for the Daily Mirror. They moved in just before Christmas 1962, when there was a very large downfall of snow, filling the lane to the house and mill for a week or more. They sold up after 20 odd years. The next owner sold us the land. After that, Mr. and Mrs. Dyball are the present owners and they have got the Water Wheel and Mill back in working order.

Trip on the Bluebell Railway

18th July 2015. My afternoon trip with the Forget-me-Nots on the Bluebell Railway, from Sheffield Park to East Grinstead and back, brought so many memories back to me. I am sure I could fill a book.

As Derek drove me up to the Station, I thought of the times that I had cycled up the road in all weathers, sometimes on my own, at other times with school pals, Steve Bentley, Dave Claridge, Roger Mepham, Jack Pickwell and Mary Burns. There were also two more from Danehill, going to Lewes School, Vi Hemsley and Alan Huggett.

Making my way through the booking hall to the platform, I could still see Mr. Perkins, the Station Master, watching to see that we went over the bridge to the platform on the other side and not just crossing the lines. I sat on the seat with friends and then Vi, the Birthday Girl, came and sat beside me. We went back years then when her husband used to work in the office of the Timber Yard next to the Goods Yard; there was a Branch line that went right into the Timber Yard.

The train pulled in and we got on and found a seat. The guard blew his whistle and off we go, over the River Ouse, with Wapsbourne Wood on the left and Coleham on the right, then through Ketches Farm with fields both sides of the line, on our way to Horsted Keynes. It was here that other school pals used to join us from Ardingly. The man that was giving us a running commentary said that the Bluebell Railway was now going to open that Branch line to Haywards Heath. As we passed Freshfield Holt

I thought of a young couple who had left their wedding reception at The Sloop one Saturday night in the wind and rain and walked up the railway line; but at Horsted Station all that was found of them was a raincoat on the engine's front buffer.

Moving on from Horsted Keynes I noticed that it was not a double track now, only a single line. Then into the half mile tunnel and out to what used to be West Hoathly Station, now only the brickwork of the old platform. Then on to Kingscote where we stopped for a few minutes – I was able to drink my cup of tea then, without spilling it. Now over the viaduct and into East Grinstead, not the real station but a long platform beside Sainsbury's car park. We stopped there for 20 minutes so that, if you wished, you could stretch your legs and also in order to let the engine get from the front to the back. Lesley shouted "All Aboard!" No, someone is missing! Found at last and on our way.

So on the way back to Sheffield Park I just sat there looking out of the window, with a piece of Vi Perrin's 100th Birthday Cake, thinking what it used to look like seventy years ago. Yes, the Stations were clean and tidy, the track was well maintained, just like it was when it was all done by hand, by Mr. Scott, Mr. Carter, Mr. Ticehurst and Mr. Whiting, who all lived in the Railway Cottages. A lot of the farm land, close to the railway line, looked to me that it was not farmed as it used to be. I only saw, close to the line, one field of oats and as for the Woods, they were mostly overgrown.

Ah well, that's me, living in the past again!

Fletching Home Guard

SEPTEMBER 2015

Going back now seventy five years, May 1940 (panic stations, the Germans are diving into France), this was when the L.D.V. (Local Defence Volunteers) began. "Will all those wishing to join please register at the local Police Station". Lots of people signed on but what shall we do with them? What a shambles. It all got sorted out in the end. Armbands with L.D.V. were given to each member and night duty was arranged for a few volunteers to be on watch at Piltdown each night.

Soon things changed. It became the Home Guard under the Army. Fletching HG became D Company 17th Battalion Royal Sussex Regiment. Their Headquarters were the Reading Room, Sheffield Green. Every night from then on, one NCO and five Privates stood guard from 10.00pm to 6.00am.

Sunday morning there was drill (under a Regular Army Officer and an NCO), either in the Park or at the Railway Station, which we might have to defend if the enemy did get here (THE RAILWAY BRIDGE the River and Road Bridge). When Pill Boxes were built around the Station and Bridges we thought "That's great" but we changed our minds when we saw the Flame Throwers we knew nothing about.

15th September 2015

Just sitting alone to think hard, as the old memory goes back in time. The first thing I knew of Stanley Peter Setford was a photo of him in the News Chronicle, opening the very large gates of North Lodge to let Queen Mary pass through to visit Mrs. Soames at Sheffield Park's Big House. It was never quite big enough to be called a Mansion, but to us it really was! That must have been something like 1935 or 6.

His next move was to come and live at The Forge, next to Vigoes Farmhouse, just separated by the orchard. He very often used to run down for my mother to go up to his mum for an afternoon cup of tea and a chat. (He would always sing: "Little old lady, time for tea.") His first school was a morning class at Miss Bott's − I think it was over the Baker's in Fletching Street − before going to the local school. He was there until he left at 14. He really did want to go and work for Mr. Griffiths at Splaynes Green, but his dad got him to work with him and his uncles at Northall Farm and Coleham. He was not a very happy boy. I am sure he would have liked to do his own thing.

When he got his first car, a Morris 8, he began to get about − Badminton, Old Time Dancing and Cattle Markets. He also got involved in some Civil Defence Group at Crowborough and did very well. It was on one of his Saturday night dancing trips that he went to Henfield. That was the start of things to come − he met Gladys Tear and her friend Margaret.

After their marriage at Henfield, Stan managed to acquire the piece of land (THE ALLOTMENT) between The Forge and Gable Cottage and got Mr. Gilliam of Nutley to build him a bungalow. When Stan and Glad moved in they gave a party for family and friends, with a large bag at the front door and a notice " Put your troubles in the bag at the front door and come in and have a good time". It most certainly was!

Stan's Mother died on Christmas Eve, 24th December 1967, aged 71. Stan's Dad died, being taken in an ambulance to Lewes Hospital, on 18th February 1984, aged 96. The Forge stood empty for some time and Stan and Glad moved to Coleham Cottage. Laramie was bought by Tony Welfare.

After a short time Stan and Glad moved to Forest Lodge (happy days!) It was Stan who moved the Clay Pigeon Shoot from the Sheffield Arms well away from the Fletching Road to a field close to Sheffield Forest, a fair distance from any houses. Close to the Shoot he invested in a small shed, doing snacks, tea and coffee for the gun owners. Soon shooters were coming from farther away; this was the beginning of the Northall Clay Pigeon Shoot.

After his Morris 8 he had many different means of transport: a Rover car, Land Rover, big red Van, and a Pickup Truck - this was his Best Buy; Glad and Stan went to Scotland a few times in this. He was all for selling up one day and buying a farm in Scotland. Of course, this never happened. While Glad was in Haywards Heath hospital Stan had skin trouble with his legs, but did not see his doctor. Had he done so it would have saved his life. Ian found him dead on the bathroom floor, 18th June 1992, aged 64. Fletching church was packed solid at his funeral, with his deer stalker hat laid on the coffin.

SADLY MISSED BY ALL .

Roy in Hospital

Firstly, I would like to thank all of you that sent me cards and get-well messages while I was in the Princess Royal Hospital all through August.

My appointment was for 11.00 a.m. I arrived at 10.40. Mr. Edmondson was waiting for me and he said "I have studied your X-Rays; they are in quite a mess and at your age the op. will be 50-50. If you would like to say 'No' I quite understand." Well, here we are once again! I must say that the first few days in Intensive Care were a bit iffy. After a few more days I was moved to a single room in Albourne Ward, where I stayed for 4 to 5 days. My second day a Dr. James came to remove the old dressings from my leg and hip and put new ones on. We chatted and he told me that his parents still lived in Nutley and he first went to school in Nutley and then to Uckfield. In his teens he used to visit a young girl by the name of Philippa Mann and she lived at Woolpack Farm – did I know of it? (Of course!) Yes, he came to see me a number of times, just to remind him of his younger days.

Also, there was a gentleman that first came to the Ward, visiting each one of us, saying he was an R.C. member. An interesting man. He said that every morning he took his two children to Fletching School and that he knew of the Priest-in-Charge and what a very good school it is. I told him my children and grandchildren went there. He left this Text with me, *A Prayer for Life*, which at the time was so helpful.

A Prayer for Life

Dear Lord Jesus, as the sun rises each morning, never let me forget that you are always there for me. You came down from Heaven and became like us, suffered as we do, then died on the cross to atone for our sins. Help me to be more like you, to prepare myself for an eternal life with you in Heaven.

The Forge – Sheffield Park

When I came to live at Vigoes Farm in March 1934 the Forge, our next door neighbour, was still shoeing horses and the Blacksmith was Mr. Norton. I am not sure what happened then, but our new neighbours were Mr. and Mrs. Setford and Stan. There was no more noise of the hammer banging on the anvil: maybe I was away with my Grandparents. Anyway, it all became a long-standing friendship, more so throughout the War. Mr. Bert Setford died on the 18th February 1984, after which the Forge was empty for some time until it was taken over by Tim Jefferies, grandson of the Green Shield millionaire.

The Ram

In the late Twenties and early Thirties, just after 7 o'clock most mornings, you would see old Mr. Burley (who lived in North Lodge, Searles Estate and who was father of Bill Burley, a keeper on the Sheffield Park Estate), walking along the road past Woolpack Farmhouse and through a gateway leading eventually to Middle Field. "What does he do, Dad?" said I. "He looks after the water that supplies Searles house and farm; he goes to check the Ram in the field." (Six-year-old me thought he meant a male sheep!)

It was not until we moved to Vigoes Farm in March 1934 that I learned what sort of ram Dad had spoken about. There is a stream that runs from Sheffield Mill to the lakes in Sheffield Park, dividing Vigoes from Northall. Going over the stream into part of Sheffield Forest where it was boggy, you would find a small brick built square, about 4'0" x 4'0", covered by a concrete slab. Inside you could hear a little noise, like a beat. This was what is known as the Ram. It pushed water from a good spring (which also had a large bed of watercress) up to a large tank close to what was then Forest Lodge. The water could then flow down in pipes to provide water for the stock at Northall Farm.

Many years later when a gas pipe was entrenched through both farms, the Gas Company must have cut through the main water vein, causing the spring to partly dry up. (Luckily by then mains water was in the area.) A great deal of water followed the gas pipe line into the fields of Vigoes. Mr. Setford and I spoke to the Gas Company, but we got nowhere.

The workings of a Ram are really quite simple if you have got a good flow of water into the container that supplies any other one with a valve. When full it pushes the water into a storage tank – then it starts all over again!

Ghosts of Christmases Past

FEBRUARY 2016

Here we go – the start of another year! Christmas 2015 has slipped away. Nothing like the Christmas that used to be when I was a boy, at least 90 years ago. We thought we were rich if we found sixpence in the toe of our sock hanging on the bed rail, and if you were lucky enough to find a silver coin in your Christmas Pud, worth three pence, Mother would say "You can put that in your Post Office savings book."

Another Christmas delight was in the time my Father was sawing logs for the fire. He would save a very large oak log so that, at some time, he would drill one-inch holes right through this log. Christmas Eve this was put on the open fire so that we could watch the flames coming through the holes, lighting the way for Father Christmas or Santa Claus. Before the log was reduced to ashes, up those stairs you must go and to sleep very quick!

I remember one present that I had which gave me hours of enjoyment – a Drawing Book with crayons of different colours, possibly bought in Woolworth's for a few pence.

Whatever would my great-grandchildren think of that to-day? How times have changed!

Mavis Wingrove

MARCH 2016

At Christmas time 2015 there was another sad loss to the Parish; Mavis Wingrove. I don't know exactly when we first met, but it must have been a few years before September 1939. She lived with her parents, Mr. and Mrs. Monk, her two sisters, Joyce and Beryl, and a younger brother, Tony, in a house opposite the Rose and Crown.

When World War II started Mavis joined the WRAF. Later in life she married Vic, who ran a little Dance Band. They often played in the School for the Saturday Night Dance – no Village Hall in those days! Their daughter, Sarah, used to come with others and play at Vigoes.

All in the past now. Sadly, all the folks I used to know in Fletching keep saying Goodbye.

(Mavis died on the 22nd December 2015 aged 95 and her Funeral Service took place in Fletching Church on Friday 22nd January 2016)

Question ?

The new film of the Home Guard and the old television series must have cost a great deal, but you never saw a PAY PARADE, did you?

What's more, didn't the real Home Guard serve for four years without pay? What a grand body of men and women – four years' service!

Late Members of the Forget-me-Nots

APRIL 2016

Irene and I, with Gladys Setford, joined the Club in 1982, but Stan Setford said "Oh, no! I am far too young!"

Eileen Howe and Jennifer Elson were in charge then. I think one of my first outings was a Coach Trip to the Orchards of Kent – plus a farmhouse tea!

Since then things are so different, there have been so many changes in the Parish, so now, just for a moment, let us remember some of the real people of the Fletching Forget-me-Nots:

Mrs. Morley, Lesley's Grandmother; Mrs. Beech; Mrs. Constable; Penny's Mum, Hilda Palmer; Joan Kilby; and our piano player, José Thompson; George and Ron Horscroft; Fred and Ada Gladman; Bill and Eileen Howe; Ivy Funnell; Kay Collins; Fred and Audrey Stevens; Ron and Pauline Cash; Eddie and Edie Moore.

>We are the Members, who meet twelve times a year
>
>For games and trips, not forgetting good Christmas cheer.
>
>Although we are all getting quite old
>
>And our aching bones can't stand the cold,
>
>On every month on the third Thursday
>
>We get together, have a laugh and chatter away,
>
>A very nice cup of tea and lovely cakes too.
>
>Then Lesley takes charge, oh what a to-do!

She tells us next month what we ought to bring.

Someone plays the piano and we have to sing.

We tidy up the Hall and get on our way

Saying Cheerio to friends for a lovely day.

Sheffield Forest

MAY 2016

Now which of you, who have made a new home in the Parish of Fletching, have taken the time to stroll in Sheffield Forest?

It covers quite a large area, nearly all of it has been replanted by the Forestry Commission after the Estate was sold in 1954. There must be at least six ways into it, with most of the Rides meeting at Sheffield Mill, which has many years of history. I am sure I have walked all the Paths and Rides in my time, not only for pleasure, but as a worker, or as a Beater when the Soames family had a Pheasant Shoot, or when the Head Keeper arranged a Fox or Rabbit Shoot. Sometimes there would be a Pigeon Shoot, where four or five guns were put at different places in the Forest. Many times, when walking through the undergrowth, I came across an overgrown deep hole, or pit. I mentioned this to one of the Keepers (Mr. Will Burley). He said it could be where a terrier dog had been dug out with a badger or a fox.

I have learned differently now. They were Saw Pits, when large Oak, Beech and Ash trees were cut down and sawn into long planks and the cord wood or branches were used in making charcoal.

Rock or Iron stone was dug in the Forest, taken to the Mill where the Water Wheel drove the bellows to keep the charcoal fires melting the iron rock to get the iron ore. This was then transported to Blackboys by Horse and Cart.

The Day War Broke Out

JUNE 2016

Many years ago, when you turned the radio on, you might have heard Rob Wilton say "The Day War broke out ……" Well, who can remember what they were doing on that Sunday, the 3rd September, 1939 at 11 o'clock?

Yes, I can. I was standing by the side of the Pond next to the road at Woolpack Farm, using the rotary pump to fill the tanks in the Cattle Yard for the cows to drink. After that, took a steady walk through Sheffield Forest to the Mill and then across the fields to Vigoes, just in time for Sunday lunch.

Standing outside the back door was my Dad, my Uncle Nelson, Bill Ockenden the Herdsman, and Mr. Bert Setford from the Forge next door. Both Dad and Nelson had served in France, 1914-1918. Bill had done 12 years in the Royal Marines, also in France and the Battle of Jutland, on board the *Warspite* (I think, not sure), Mr. Setford being the eldest (not sure). They were talking about their War and how this War was going to be so different. The Top Brass would not be dining well behind the front line and saying Send this or that Regiment over the top.

Monday morning, no change. Up at 4.30, milk the cows, breakfast and away with the lorry to exchange empty churns for full ones from the Farms. Nutley to Fletching, Sheffield Green and Furners Green, then stop-start to the Mid-Sussex Creamery so that Mr. B. Setford could deliver some of his milk to the ladies who would be waiting for us with their cans and jugs. When we got to Railway Cottages the Air Raid siren went. When we got to Dairy and Albert Cottages the jugs were there, but no ladies. It wasn't till next day that we heard that they had all run into Wapsbourne Wood!

Ploughing

Who, in this day and age, likes to go to a Ploughing Match? I do! Those who are competing do take pride in their work, not like many ploughmen of to-day with a large tractor and a five-or-six reversible plough, who follow the hedge or fence line and keep going till the job is completed. No straight, shining furrows.

My Father, with his two horses and single-furrow plough, was well satisfied if he had turned over one acre in a day.

When I was only four years old he made me a little wooden seat on the plough. I would get on as the horses started to go down the field and jump off as they got to the end, to swing the plough over onto the wing, to turn round and go back up the other furrow. As I got older he had a tractor and a two-furrow plough and then it became my turn to do the ploughing. I well remember my first effort, marking out the headland; that is you follow the outside of the field all around, about four yards in ploughing a Flit furrow, then you mark out your cants; when you finish two cants you should leave a very straight furrow across the field, so that a rabbit running down it would not knock its hips!

At my first attempt I had left some odd bits not ploughed, so, as Dad was away at the Haywards Heath Market, I ran home for a spade....

Another time, ploughing the last outside round of the field, I got the Ransom trailer plough locked up under a very large Oak root. This made the old Fordson start to rear, so foot on the clutch very quick. As it would not reverse I had to unhitch and pull the plough out from the back end.

Later in life, when we changed the two cart horses and the Fordson tractor for two little grey Fergies with all the hydraulic implements, farming was making progress and life got easier.

Reg Lingham (Roy's uncle) and Arthur Burley

Agricultural Shows in Sussex

AUGUST 2016

By now the 2016 South of England Show will have been forgotten and the 2017 Show will be well at an advanced stage.

Now let's go back in time, before the Tunbridge Wells and the Sussex Show joined forces and had a permanent Showground at Ardingly.

The first Show I went to was the one at Tunbridge Wells. My Uncle George was showing some of his canaries and budgies. We went by train from Forest Row station and it was quite a long walk to the Showground from the Wells station. He was very pleased as he took a few 1sts, 2nds and 3rds.

My next was the Sussex Show at Cooksbridge. I went with my Father and other Farmers in an old Morris van. On arrival at the Showground we all remarked on the smell of something burning. Later we found out that experiments were being tried out in converting new-mown grass into pellet cubes. A few years on most Dairy farmers were feeding grass pellets. (Times have changed – not spoken of now). On the way home the van ran out of petrol. We all pushed it the last 200 yards to the garage at the King's Head, Chailey.

The Sussex Show at Midhurst was held on the Cowdray Estate. By then I had passed my driving test so, with a few friends, I hired a car from Mr. Channing at Furner's Green Garage. It was the first time I had ever seen a Polo Match. It was a very hot day and, being so warm, a little time was spent in the Beer Tent. I would not have been able to drive home in this day and age!

When another Sussex Show was held at Hassocks (Keymer, truthfully) it was a working day out for me in our lorry. I had to take and help show some boars and gilts for the Hunt and Butt

Pedigree herd of Large Whites from Tanyard Farm, Furner's Green. They were very pleased with the results.

Another year and the Sussex Show was held at Sidley, not far from Bexhill. Mr. Hunt asked me to take, very early, three prize gilts to the Show and he would follow me with his large White Boar, in his car and trailer.

When we arrived at the Show and got all his pigs safely penned in, I returned home as we were haymaking. I managed to get back to collect the pigs by 8.30 p.m. Now that's another story ......Arriving back at the Showground and on letting the ramp down ready for loading, two men came to give a hand. One said to me "Capt. Hunt would also like you to take his 'Supreme Champion Boar' home as well." I put the Boar in first and penned it in, so that the gilts were away from him (good thinking) and then went and found Bill Hunt in the Members' Tent with friends. "Ah, Roy," he said, the words a little slurred, "would you tell my wife I might be a little late coming home." Back to Sheffield Mill Farm, unloaded, pigs safely away, message delivered to Mrs. Hunt, home to bed for me. At 11.45 p.m. my phone rings – Mrs. Hunt: "Bill is not home yet, so I have rung the police." Capt. Hunt was found next morning in a village pub, somewhere in Kent. "Must have taken the wrong road", that's all he said.

The Edenbridge Show is so much larger, now that it has moved closer to the A22 at Blindley Heath. It is mostly held on the Bank Holiday week-end.

Our Christmas treat for the wife and me used to be a day's trip to visit the Smithfield Fat Stock Show, where some of the butchers would pay a very large amount of money for top prize animals. After that, a nice hot tea and a good theatre show. To us that was a day well spent, just to have got away from the daily farm routine. Now I am not sure of the year, but it was in the very early fifties when we were going to London for the Smithfield Show and it was very foggy. We caught the 7 a.m. train at Sheffield Park station and when we got to London it was quite dark with the fog and smog; you could hardly see anything in front of you. The newspaper sellers were shouting "Smog has closed the Smithfield Show, the animals have been sent home". We had to make the best of a bad day's outing and after that we always called it "going up the smoke".

All finished now, hardly any coal fires these days and very few Coal Merchants. One time of day most Villages had one. Fletching Coal Yard was at the back of The Griffin.

Stan Setford and Roy Lingham

Memorable Dates

Not so very long ago one of my Grandsons, Ben, with his girl friend, paid me a visit and said: "Dot this date down in your diary – September the third. It's the day we are going to get wed, in the same church in Fletching where you and Nan walked down the aisle on 16th April 1947."

Ben was born at Vigoes and at five years old started school here, but he had to leave when his parents went to live at Worth Abbey, where his father worked.

However did they think that I would ever forget that particular date? 3rd September 1939 was the day War broke out. It is truly stuck in my mind, like all those other folk of my age. There were so many mates, friends and young people who never, ever reached the age of 21.

Those two dates are truly embedded in the old "Noddy Box".

3rd September, 2016

In this grand old church of a great many years

There has been lots of laughter and so many tears,

So for all of us that are gathered here to-day

To wish Claire and Ben good luck in every way.

Now, for Ben, Claire becomes his lovely wife

And, with the Blessing of Our Lord, a long and happy life.

With their two children, jumping for joy,

Lovely Ruby, the girl, and cheeky Finn, the boy.

So their love in the future will have to be strong

Because, for both of them, Happiness is their true love song.

My Grandfather's advice to us, when we got wed,

Was "You must solve your problems before going to bed."

I wrote this little poem at the request of my Grandson, Ben, who also said would I read it in church? I must say I did manage it, but my mind was really going back Sixty Nine years, when Irene and I stood there.

I should very much like to thank Lucy for the way she conducted the Wedding Service and also for giving up her time to come back to Fletching to do the honours.

When it was all over and the photos taken (pity the sun did not shine) then, quite a surprise to us all, a small helicopter landed close by to take them to the Reception at Worth Abbey. We should have guessed, because they both work for Virgin Airline.

When we all got to the Abbey there were more photos, drinks, a hearty meal, and Toast to the Bride and Groom, and Disco for the young later in the evening.

We send Claire and Ben, Roy's grandson, our best wishes for every happiness in their future together. **Editors**

Those Were The Days – Harvest Time

The date: 2/10/2016. The time: 19.30. The Fletching Church Harvest Festival is now over for another year and this year not a family member helping with the plough. I am not sure of my first time (many years ago).

Now, after watching *Country File* this evening on TV, all the Harvest has been safely gathered in. What a difference it is now to when I was first old enough to help my father at Woolpack Farm. It was a field of winter oats going up the hill to Wilmshurst. I had to ride the third horse that was hitched in front of the two horses pulling the binder. Hence me being a little bow legged!

To-day, when the weather permits it, all finished in one go; for us, it took weeks. First, a man with a scythe cut the corn around the edge of the field, about a yard-and-a-half. This had to be bundled up by hand and stood to one side; this was really so that the horse and binder did not waste any.

When the field was cut and all the sheaves had been stacked up, next they were loaded on to a wagon and taken to the Farm and a stack was made. This had to be thatched to keep it dry. Later on, when the thatcher came all the corn bagged and the straw all bundled up, or, if loose, another stack built. Now to-day, with all the modern machinery, it takes just two or three workers, when in those days a dozen or more hard-working men, women and children, for just a few pence, for long hours. Say no more.

The Sheffield Arms

DECEMBER 2016

The Forget-me-Nots Outing on Thursday, 15th September, 2016 was a very nice Tea at The Sheffield Arms – sorry, my mistake, Trading Boundaries. To Derek, Ann and myself it was like going back in time.

What a difference a few years can make. My nearly eighty years living in the Farm next door, which, at one time, years ago, went with the Hotel. It was also a place where they changed horses for the coach which went from Croydon, via East Grinstead, Lewes and Brighton. Of course, this all stopped when Lord Sheffield helped pay for the LBSC railway which was built from East Grinstead to Lewes.

When I came to live at Vigoes from Woolpack, the Tenants of the Sheffield Arms were Mr. and Mrs. Edwards and their son, Frank. He went to the same school as I did, but he was much older than me. During the Summer months Mrs. Edwards sold afternoon teas in the Pavilion at the Cricket Ground in the Park on Sundays, when the Gardens were open to the public. They moved on to another hotel in Lewes (sadly, Frank lost his life at Dunkirk). Next were Messrs. Boyes, then Mr. and Mrs. Ganders, followed by Mr. Swaby. They left soon after the Second World War started and Mr. and Mrs. Harry Grace stayed till 1948. During their stay the tennis grass court and bowling green disappeared in the "Dig for Victory".

Following them, came several Managers – Sutton, Kimberley, Salmon, Sargent, Wake, (Mr. and Mrs. Frank Wake took the Rose and Crown), then the Claytons. There was one more tenant before the 99-year lease ended. The Sheffield Arms was then empty for a year and a half. After that it changed hands a few times, but now that Mr. and Mrs. Clifford own it, things have changed for the better.

Now, as the old memory is beginning to fade away, I think I had better jot down a few bits I can still remember of my time living next to the Sheffield Arms.

For many years it always had two Dart Teams. The Monday Night Team used to play in the Mid Sussex League which covered many pubs in and around Haywards Heath. The Friday Team played in the Forest Row and District League. We also played darts for the Coronation Cup, given by Mrs. Soames. Teams came from The Peacock, The Piltdown Man, The Griffin, The Rose and Crown, The Sloop and The Sheffield Arms. Most of us know that The Piltdown Man was The Lamb and is now The Lamb again. But who can remember The Star, close to the Monkey Puzzle? Also, The Old Surrey and Burstow Hunt, meeting outside the Sheffield Arms. What a wonderful sight, all the hounds walking about in and out of the crowds. Then, once a year, the Little Fair on the Common opposite the Hotel, with swings and a hand-turned roundabout, and, in Pound Farm's field, running races, sack and wheelbarrow, egg and spoon. NO MORE – just memories.

3rd September 1939: so many changes. The Welsh Regiment that moved into the Park, the morning work and walk for the few, plus a pint or two with their Mascot, the Goat, in the Regiment's colours. They moved. In came the "Pandas" an English regiment. After that, two Canadian regiments, the French Canadians and the Cape Breton Highlanders. The beer was too strong for them – there were fights among them, as the Park was divided, one lot to The Sheffield Arms, and the other to The Griffin or The Rose and Crown. War over, and a few of the local girls married the lads and went back to Canada to live.

After the 99-year lease ended and The Sheffield Arms stood empty for eighteen months, fresh owners, new ideas. First, it was to be a large motel, but NO – the money ran out. Next, a Night Club with a disco: all OK until a coach load from Brighton and one from London had a disagreement. One coach went up in flames and fights; that was the end of that. Another owner disappeared – all the money gone in debts. I think I will just let sleeping dogs lie.

Roy Lingham Remembers

Christmas 2016: It was my Ninety-fourth. Now it is just a thing of the past, but I can still remember some of the old ones.

1925: Dad's Yule Log – the large piece of wood he had made holes in, so that as we sat around the fire we watched the flames coming out of the holes.

1929: My first bicycle and a bike ride with Dad to Uckfield Picture House to see Buck Jones in a Western.

1930: A Christmas Party, where we children could only look at the large iced cake, being told it was for the grown-ups' party the next day. A few moans and girlie tears.

1934: My first Christmas at Vigoes Farm. Also, the loss of my Grandad and Aunt Eve.

1937: My School Dance and Leavers Party.

1939: What's on the cards…..? Who knows?

1942: Fletching Home Guard. A get-together in the Sheffield Arms for a Christmas Dinner, Rabbit Stew and Xmas Pud. Keepers and Poachers, the rabbits; and fruit for the pudding by the Canadian Troops.

1943: My cousin's bomber missing over Germany and we did not hear until March 1944 that he was a POW, Stalag Luft III. He returned home in '45 a bag of bones; was in one of those forced marches, caught up by the Russians, but, with two others, managed to get to the Yanks.

1947: April 16th, my marriage to Irene and our first Christmas.

As the family grew up, more parties at Vigoes.

2001: My first at Newick.   And...

2014: In Brighton Hospital. Also the sad loss of Irene.

The Times They Are a-Changing

MARCH 2017

We all know that things and times are changing. I still think of some of the old folk that would turn up at different times.

Like the man you used to see in the Springtime, pushing his homemade two-wheeled trolley.

Then there was a man known to all as Spot Leopard. He used to follow the Thatcher around, so maybe the Farmer would give him a job, like bagging up chaff, or cavel raking.

Also, there was a lady who used to travel around with her belongings in an old pram. She was known as Old Meg. It was said that at some time she lived in a cave just off Buckham Hill. It was also said that she was from a well-to-do gentry family.

All these folk had good relations with all the local Coppers, who also got some good information.

Then there were the gypsies who came round selling clothes pegs and painted wooden flowers; and the old roadsters that travelled all over the country, going from one Workhouse to another. If they called at someone's house where perhaps the lady felt sorry for them and perhaps gave them a cup of tea and a piece of cake, they would leave a mark on a bush or tree beside the road, for others to know.

Sometimes on our way home from School, while getting close to East Grinstead Railway Station and the high bank of earth, nearly opposite East Grinstead Workhouse, carrying the railway line to Forest Row, we would see a Tramp sitting there. We used to think the tramps were waiting for opening time.

No, they were on the earth bank burying their few coins which they had put in a cocoa tin. If they had money on them, it was taken away to help pay for their time in the Workhouse.

The Common

APRIL 2017

Once again chatting with Eric, the Common when we were young lads became the subject. It really was Manorial Waste, stretching from Lodge Hill to Paygate. Both sides of the road, from the Sheffield Arms cross-roads up over Lodge Hill, was all grass land while, when looking South, on the left was one very large Beech tree and a very tall Fir (both good for climbing). On the other side, the stone-built signpost. Sometimes the Sheffield Estate would let cattle graze it, all looked after by two workers.

Now going North, when the Dairy Cows fed it off, Mr. Tester from Pound Farm and Don Lingham from Vigoes Farm had an agreement that both herds of cows would feed the grass off the same day. So that they were kept apart, Pound on the left, Vigoes on the right, there were three of us stationed up the road, Bill and Jack Tester and yours truly. It worked very well – not a lot of traffic in those days. Quite often folks from Winter Cottage (now Little Manor) and Yew Tree Cottage would cross the road with the yokes and two buckets, to get their water from the separate wells on the Common.

There were six wells, all on the same under-spring water vein:- One on the opposite side of the road for Paygate; the next one in front of Vigoes Cottage (now knocked into one - Greystones); another further down the Common for Winter Cottage, three cottages at Chequers (now one house), Three Gables made larger and then the Estate workers' allotment – they used the water for plants. The next well was just outside the Forge House back door; one more at the back of Vigoes Cottage and the other one on the left-hand side of the back door to the Kitchen of the Sheffield Arms.

After the Estate Sale Stanley Setford had a bungalow built, (which was later knocked down and now there is a large house, Yaffles Rest). Mains water was then laid on.

The Forge

MAY 2017

Many years ago, when the land was worked by horses, each Village had a Smithy (or should I have said a Blacksmith?) working in the Forge. Fletching Forge was at Splaynes Green, the Blacksmith was Mr. Frank Packham and his understudy was Mr. Munday. I did not like him because when he shod our horses he always used a Twitch. Now I can hear you say "What is a Twitch?" It is a strong bit of cord with a loop fixed to a handle-shaped piece of wood, about 9" long. The loop was put over the flesh part of the horse's nose and twisted up very tight. (Also used by Vets).

The Sheffield Park Estate Forge was just a few yards from Vigoes Farm and the sound of the hammer banging on the anvil could be clearly heard. Mr. Jim Norton was the Blacksmith, but he moved away in 1934 as tractors were beginning to take over. It was then that a new range of Mobile Blacksmiths arrived, going to the horses, not the horses coming to them.

Herbert Setford then moved into the Forge House, with his wife and son, Stanley. The Estate then transferred the tenancy of the Forge to H. Setford & Sons, of Northall and Colham Farms.

Both Mr. and Mrs. Setford lived their lives out at the Forge. Mrs. Alice Setford passed away Christmas Eve 1967, aged 71. Mr. Bert Setford lived until February 18th 1984, aged 94. Stanley, after the War, married a Land Girl from Henfield, Miss Gladys Tear. They first lived in a bungalow built on the old Allotments at Sheffield Green; then in one of two cottages in Ketches Lane; finally, they moved to Forest Lodge. Sadly, both did not have a very long life. Stanley Setford died on June 18th 1992, aged 64 and Gladys Setford on January 22nd 2000, aged 73. Both very sadly missed by Fletching Parish friends.

Robert Whitham

Robert will be sadly missed by all of us from the Forget-me-Nots. He became the Club Treasurer after Beryl Browne. Mick and Beryl left to live in Horam.

Things changed. Once a year Robert gave us all a full account of the Club's Financial Accounts. This was something that he was very keen to do.

Also, if the Club had no Outings, entertainment, or a Speaker, there were always Robert's Quizzes to fill the gap. I remember Penny's Mum was nearly always the winner (Bless her.)

Robert died on March 29th, aged 86 and his funeral was -held on April 28th 2017 in Fletching Parish Church.

21226014R00079

Printed in Poland
by Amazon Fulfillment
Poland Sp. z o.o., Wrocław

Roy's Rambles around Fletching

memories of a Sussex Parish

by

Roy P. Lingham